MONS

CW00411481

Art work: Matt Bradshaw (page 4), Heather Paxton (page 30), and
Denis St. John (page 64)

Contributors: Stephen R. Bissette, Eric Messina, Steve Fenton, Matt
Bradshaw, Tim Paxton, Troy Howarth, John Harrison, and Jason Cook

Timothy Paxton, Editor & Design Demon
Steve Fenton, Editor & Info-wrangler
Tony Strauss, Edit-fiend
Brian Harris, El Publisher de Grand Poobah

Volume 4 / Issue #10 / October 2014 / 1st Printing

Editorializing

Pictured here seated next to a spooky devil is the Topstone Company's rubber mask known as "The Ghoul". This was the mask I most frequently purchased for an assortment of Halloween or 8mm film projects. It's too bad my collection eventually decayed into a sticky mass of stinking latex. These vintage masks are now highly collectible, and go for big bucks on eBay. (Photo: *monsterkidclassichorrorforum.yuku.com/reply/857282/Topstone-masks#*)

Other than the addition of 30 extra bonus pages (our typical issue runs 70 pages), this Halloween edition of *Monster!* is really no more special than any of the previous nine. It just so happens that Halloween falls in October and monsters play a large part in its celebration. What's odd is that this spooky holiday, for the most part, originated in the United States, but it is now celebrated with zeal the world over. Folks have argued that it is rooted to the ancient pagan order of druids and nature-worship in general. Sure, why not. Then there are the wild theories from those obsessed with all things Lovecraftian that "All Hallow's Eve" is older and has something to do with the Elder Gods. I'll mention something about that later on. Whatever the case to be argued, Halloween is one night that I loved as a child, and still do to some degree as a grey-haired gentleman of 52. When I was 10 years old I got a photo of myself on the cover of *The Oberlin News Tribune* wearing my two-headed monster costume. I fashioned the get-up together with a pair of rubber masks I bought from our local Ben Franklin's store. I thought I did

a great job with "The Ghoul" and "Male Vampire" masks (I took my inspiration from photos I had seen of Anthony M. Lanza's **THE INCREDIBLE TWO-HEADED TRANSPLANT** in a 1971 issue of either *Famous Monsters* or *The Monster Times*).

I won an award at our town's annual Halloween parade: "Funniest costume"…I was *not* happy!

That sniggering on the part of *The News Trib* didn't stop me from continuing my tradition of creating other oddball Halloween costumes. Most of the time it was a combination of store-bought masks and a lot of imagination. A little later on a family friend gave me a copy of Warren's fabulous *Do-it-yourself Monster Make-up Handbook* magazine (written and illustrated by the late, great Dick Smith), a book on the life of Lon Chaney, and a small starter kit full with grease paint, non-flexible collodion, a vial of stage blood, a pint of latex, and two braids of theatrical hair. I was set for the rest of my life as a makeup man for future monster movies! I never did get into creating cinematic creatures for a living, but every once in a while I do dress up for the holiday.

Monster movies and makeup—For me, that is what Halloween is all about. So, every issue of *Monster!* is a special one (*Damn straight! – SF* ☺). Just for kicks this ish, there is a wonderful article from our valued Australian correspondent John Harrison on his Don Post collection. John's piece is followed by a reprint of an old 1959 issue of *Popular Science* that featured a fun little article on Don Post and his company. Personally I could never afford one of those Don Post creations (see page 68), and was still happy to shell out $2 for a flimsy latex three quarter (not quite full) head mask from my local Ben Franklin's store.

Halloween is about ghosts as well. Which begs the question: are ghosts monsters and do they belong in this zine? Honestly, I don't see why not (*Me neither! – SF*). They're supernatural, and they are no longer human. Sure, they aren't corporal creatures (unless you encounter dualistic entities like the monster from Vinod Talwar's **KHOONI PANJA** [see p.5]), but what constitutes a monster anyways? Do you actually have to be a creature in a feature to be included in these pages? Are Jason, Michael, and Freddy monsters? *Heck yea they are!* And they were the trinity of terror that was the driving force in the 1980s through the 2000s along with George Romero's zombies and the multitude of **ALIEN** clones.

WANTED! More Readers Like Heather the Vampire and Tim the Yokai (Halloween 2011)

"100% Slasher-Free": that *is* the motto of this magazine (*It's tattooed on our foreheads – SF*). The title says it all: Monster Movies Galore. All monsters and no slashers. I am not too concerned with gore. Monsters kill and sometimes eat people, and that's part of their makeup. That's were zombies came in. And werewolves. Vampires. Blobs. Aliens. (And so on and so forth…)

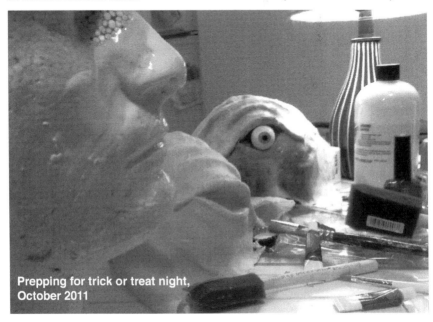

Prepping for trick or treat night, October 2011

All of the above pretty much covers the definition of monster for us. Now, there *are* borderline beasts: those creatures that some people may not really consider monsters but nevertheless are. That is where ghosts come in (see above). These are supernatural, non-human entities and therefore... monsters. You could say that zombies are a form of ghost, just as werewolves are both human and lycanthrope. People consider devils and demons monsters. If they are, then you should also include major as well as minor deities in that field.

It's human monsters that will not appear in this magazine (*Hell no! – SF*). Now, you may question the logic behind reviewing **HALLOWEEN III:**
SEASON OF THE WITCH if human monsters are a no-no. I love that film, and consider it the best of the series. But are there monsters in it? Yes and no. Sure, there are killer robots, and they are a monster of sorts. What really makes the film is the final few minutes. You don't actually *see* the ancient gods returning to our realm, but they *will* because of the actions of the kind folks behind the Silver Shamrock Halloween masks. Of course, the masks are a Don Post product, and there is that connection. Pretty flimsy you say? Maybe, but I am very happy to include it in this issue (*Me too! – SF*).

~**Tim Paxton**

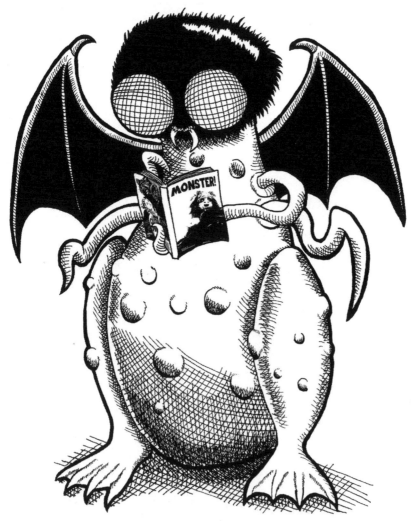

WANTED! More Readers Like Ghsbyljth-ruumpth'th McGillicutty

KHOONI PANJA

Reviewed by Tim Paxton

India, 1991. D: Vinod Talwar

This rocking little monster flick is the second-to-last such exploitative horror production to come from Mumbai-based director Vinod Talwar. I've written about Mr. Talwar's films several times. I interviewed him in *Weng's Chop* #1, and previously reviewed his films in *Monster!* #1 (**HATYARIN**, 1991) and #2 (**WOHI BHAYANAK RAAT**, 1989). Talwar has made some interesting films, and I wish he made more. The creatures that inhabit his patchwork wonders are grotesque entities indeed, more so than those of his contemporaries, the Ramsay family of fright films. They are truly corpse-like, hideous and horrifying... and they should have been films remembered today as classics in Indian cinema. But why *aren't* they? Talwar's problem seems to have been twofold, although I have never been able to get a straight answer out of him. First, I am sure there was a problem with funds, as the films, despite the director's camerawork and editing, looked

cheap. The sets seemed to be recycled, and the location shots resembled parks and other easily accessible spots for filming. Second—and this is probably the main reason—the Indian audience was simply getting tired of these types of horror films. It was 1991, and cheap, on-the-fly filmmakers like Kanti Shah were flooding the theatres with rinky-dink horror films. So too was the rise of the new generation of horror auteurs like Ram Gopal Varma, who was just getting a foothold as filmmaker with the success of his possession film **RAAT**. Monster films were on the way out and spooky ghost flicks were on the rise. Had Talwar not thrown in the towel after making what I consider his masterpiece **HATYARIN**, then I believe his name would rightly be ranked right up there with the Ramsays' in regards to their best work.

That said, now onto a film which bombed at the box office, but not in my heart: **KHOONI PANJA**, a.k.a. "Bloody Hand"…

TALWAR INTERNATIONAL PRESENTS

VINOD TALWAR'S

KHOONI PANJA

PRODUCED BY
S.K. TALWAR . VINOD TALWAR . ACHAL TALWAR
MUSIC   LYRICS   CAMERA
SURINDER KOHLI   GAUHAR KANPURI   MANISH BHATT

The three faces of evil as seen in **KHOONI PANJA** are also a trio of incongruous entities. When is a ghost a tangible thing? Why, when it's a *churail*, of course! **Top:** The spectral form of the murdered wife. **Center:** The possessed corporeal Pinky. **Bottom:** The very solid monstrous form. **Above:** A *tantrik* prepares to exorcise the young woman

As the film opens, a man and his lover are in the throes of a passionate embrace when they are surprised by the cheating husband's wife. She brandishes a gun and threatens to kill them both if they don't stop seeing each other. The table is turned when, during a struggle for the gun, it is the wife who ends up shot instead. She collapses on the ground, bleeding profusely and cursing the two scoundrels soundly before she dies. The couple are then forced to dispose of the body at a nearby graveyard, where they bribe a drunken groundsman to bury it. But the wife's reanimated corpse will have none of it, and as the husband struggles to remove it from backseat of his car, her corpse attacks the trio. Lucky for them the groundsman grabs a ceremonial sword from a nearby altar and forces the zombie into a shallow grave. Even while covered with dirt, still the living corpse reaches up out of the ground to grab at them. The groundsman lops off one of its arms (which rolls away into some bushes) with the sword, and then he plants the weapon deep into the fresh mound of earth, thus sealing the evil underneath the ground.

Roll the credits!

Years later[1] we find ourselves in the household of the lecherous husband, who has since married his lover and lives there with his extended family. Right off the bat we are introduced to the film's comedic relief, a foppish character played by actor Jagdeep. For those not familiar with Bollywood, be prepared to be annoyed! The inclusion of humorous elements into an otherwise straightforward horror film is not that uncommon in Indian cinema. It seems that this is true for most cinema in general. James Whale, a master of the macabre, felt he had to include laughs in his **BRIDE OF FRANKENSTEIN** (1935, USA), so as to offset the horror. Most of what he brewed up was subtle and campy in a sort of weird way, although he did dally in the histrionically theatrical with Una O'Connor's screeching peasant woman, Minnie. In Talwar's film the audience is allowed some lighthearted breathing room with the effeminate prancing of Jagdeep, who preaches the benefits of Michael Jackson, sashays around in swishy scarves, and giggles and bats his eyes a lot, while pretty much perpetuating the negative "gay" stereotype.[2] Such grotesque humor has

1 "Years later" is an assumption on my part, because when it comes to Indian cinema the concept and the passage of time can be very fluid. Children tend to grow up exceptionally fast, months and years melt by without any real explanation, and the confusion is compounded when many films take place in small villages or rural locations that lack any type of markers indicating what year, decades or century it might possibly be.

2 While it may be true that some of my friends who are gay do tend to get somewhat flamboyant at times, to use these buffoonish characters as the butts of jokes and ridicule in

been used since the early days of Bollywood, and it is still utilized to this day. Its inclusion is used to tone down a "thriller" or "action" film, and to keep the audience from becoming too emotional (or so I have been told). While this has been true in the past, most of the horror films made today seem to shy away from such obvious shenanigans.

Cut to a gaggle of college-age girls who are playing volleyball outside of the local cemetery with Pinky (actress Seema Vaz), the future sister-in-law of the murderous husband. A wide serve causes the ball to sail over the gate and into the grounds. Pinky offers to retrieve the ball and ends up standing on a grave. Yes, *THE* grave! The disembodied, decomposed hand belonging to the vengeful wife then attacks Pinky. She manages to wrestle free of the claw and runs from the graveyard to collapse on a nearby roadway (her friends now nowhere in sight). As it turns out, the young woman has been possessed by the ghost of the murdered wife, and she is picked up her family—who just happen to be driving by—and is taken back home. Meanwhile, her future in-laws find their framed family

photographs broken and covered in blood. Pinky's eyes glow white as she states her plans on destroying everyone associated with the family, and the game is set to play out.

The first member of the household to feel the wrath of the ghost is the lecherous house servant, who is also stinking drunk. The role of the servant is played by the late Mac Mohan, who has acted in similar parts in over 200 films (mostly small roles for numerous thrillers by Kanti Shah and other masters of low-budget exploitation); many Bollywood fans remember him for his role of Sambha in Ramesh Sippy's action flick **SHOLAY** (1975). After guzzling a quart of whisky, he attempts to molest Pinky while she is in the shower. His passion gets the better of him as the possessed girl transforms into a grotesque hulking, walking corpse. The creature's skin is red and rotten, its bald head has deep-set eyes set in a skull-like face, and its mouth is packed with long sharp teeth. The monster grabs the servant as he tries to flee, throwing him across the room and out a window into the street below.

KHOONI PANJA's monster reminds me of William Sachs' **THE INCREDIBLE MELTING MAN** (1977, USA [see *Monster!* #7]), a film which employed makeup artists Rick Baker and Greg Cannom. To save on cash, only a mask and

film is still cruel, and, sadly, typical of almost every cinema industry worldwide. There have been a few Indian horror films which "dared" to be different, Raghava Lawrence's 2011 possession horror film **KANCHANA** is one of them, whose main character is a transsexual that doesn't "act" like the typical "fairy".

For most of his films, director Vinod Talwar was forced to work with a limited budget. For **KHOONI PANJA**, he and his effects crew utilized practical effects such as this use of forced perspective to give his magical killer corpse a sense of the gigantic. A similar scene was also part of the climax for his last and most original film, **HATYARIN**

ed witch from **HATYARIN** are by far the most gruesome creatures produced by Bollywood in the 1990s.

As the film progresses, the possessed Pinky knocks off one family member after another in her monstrous form (in one scene, a young woman has the top of her head ripped off, in what was probably a gore sequence which got chopped out by Bollywood censors of the day, something not uncommon). This murder spree goes on until someone realizes that she is possessed, and a *tantrik* is called in to exorcise her. The holy man is possibly an *aghoris*: a master of the dark arts who can commune with the dead using an assortment of religious and magical paraphernalia. He sets up camp in Pinky's bedroom and begins his exorcism, she in her bed and he on the floor at his portable altar. This *aghoris* uses a special spirit jar, and, after some tough negations with the gods, he is able to extract the ghost of the murdered woman by way of the *khooni panja*, which crawls across the floor and into the jar. The wizard then seals the lid of said container with a prayer and gives it to Pinky's older brother (played by veteran actor Anil Dhawan, star of many horror films, including the cobra lady flick **NAGIN** [D: Rajkumar Kohli, 1976; reviewed in *Weng's Chop* #3], the Ramsay productions **PURANI HAVELI** [1989; reviewed in *Monster!* #4], **AJOOBA KUDRAT KA** [1991; reviewed in *Monster!* #3], plus **AAKHRI CHEEKH** [1991], and others). His duty? To bring the trapped spirit to a local temple for proper disposal. On his way he witnesses a woman being raped[4] by a group of leering men, and in stopping to help her he unwittingly breaks the jar. The spirit is rereleased, whereupon it promptly kills the wizard and continues on its rampage of revenge.

gloves were used in that film, as in Talwar's. It's a longshot, but I'd say that the director may have seen stills of the US film in various film magazines (he is still a huge fan of horror films). The special makeup for this film was probably created by "the old master" Bengali Dada[3] with assistance from the SFX team of Daya Bhai and Gordham Bhai, who also worked on **HATYARIN**. As far as creature effects go, this monster and the bloat-

---

3 Bengali Dada is the name that Talwar gives as the man responsible for all the monster make-up and designs in his films.

Not to be outdone, the remaining relatives take Pinky to another less-flamboyant holy man—a *sādhu* at the local temple—and she becomes separated from the possessing spirit. But it doesn't end there, and for the last fifteen minutes the walking corpse and the spectral form of the vengeful wife track down Pinky's future brother-in-law. We get to see a lot of the monster by the time the plot reaches its morally correct conclusion. That fact alone is what counts for me, not the extraneous padding.

The production of **KHOONI PANJA** is somewhat disjointed, and lacks much of the cohesion

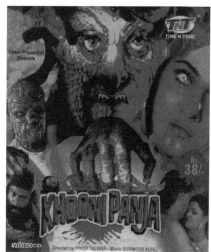

VCD set for **KHOONI PANJA**

---

4 Rape is all too common a plot element in Indian cinema of any genre (even humorous and devotional films are plagued by these sexual assaults). At a risk of sounding racist, it appears that such attacks are endemic to their society and culture.

of Talwar's final work, **HATYARIN**. It's an episodic mess of disjointed plotting, off-kilter musical numbers, insipid "kung fu" fighting, ham-fisted acting chops and overwrought family melodrama, humorous interludes, as well as stolen sequences (this time around the director borrows from, for no good reason, "The Raft" segment from **CREEPSHOW 2** [D: Michael Gornick, 1987, USA]). Despite those negative aspects, **KHOONI PANJA** does have its moments of lovely camera work, dramatic tension, and—of course!—its very cool monster; whose grotesque appearance is not unlike three other monsters which the director also developed for his films. Talwar's preference for rotting corpses is unique in Bollywood, although I have seen similar horrors before in Western movies. The monster is walking corruption personified, and it resembles the makeup effects utilized in **HATYARIN** (featuring another murdered woman who returns as a vengeful monster/ghost), complete with pulsating facial bladder effects. The mask work is similar to that used to liven up the earlier Talwar walking corpse film, **WOHI BHAYANAK RAAT**.[5]

Talwar takes the popular archetypical "woman in white" variety of Indian *bhoot* or *bhut*, or ghost, sometimes called a *daakini* or maybe a *shaakini*. Talwar puts his own spin on the tale by having the vengeful spirit possesses Pinky, and then allowing the entity to switch forms at will. One moment she is Pinky, the next she becomes the deceased wife (a.k.a. "woman in white"), and then she can become the horrid walking corpse. Talwar even enters into the weird realm of dualism when both Pinky and the monster are extant simultaneously. All of this sounds very familiar if you are hip to Chinese horror films from the 1970s through the '90s. If so, you will know what I mean when I say that India is a country where folklore, ghostly apparitions, sightings and paranormal activity is common. Despite being very different in their respective religions, there seems to be a familiar feel to the types of spectral haunting and black magic that are attached to many of the films and their plots. Granted, Chinese genre cinema of that period has gratuitous amounts of guts, gore and female nudity. That trinity of taboos rarely shows up in films from the subcontinent (where timid producers and distributors are afraid of offending India's many

---

5 Bladder effects were popular in monster films during the '80s and '90s, before usage of CG became common. Bladders were used to depict Talwar's ugly, pulsating vampire from **WOHI BHAYANAK RAAT**, which is reminiscent of Rob Bottin's onscreen transformation of Robert Picardo's Eddie Quist character in Joe Dante's **THE HOWLING** (1981), whose FX incorporated pneumatically inflatable air bladders

placed beneath latex prosthetic facial applications; while the living corpses from both **HATYARIN** and **KHOONI PANJA** reminded me of Renato Francola's makeup for Tonino Ricci's cheapozoid Italian mutant monster movie **PANIC** (*Bakterion*, a.k.a. **MONSTER OF BLOOD**, 1982).

Two of Talwar's monstrous creations had cameos in Ashim Ahluwalia's **MISS LOVELY** (2012), a film about the seedy underbelly of low-budget Bollywood horror films. This is an imagined sexy scene from a "reconstruction" of **KHOONI PANJA**. The vampire from **WOHI BHAYANAK RAAT** also made an appearance along with nods to Ramsay's movies and even a brief sequence that looks like it's from Malayalam director Baby's 1991 film **PATHI-MOONAM NUMBER VEEDU**

censors). In **KHOONI PANJA** we have magic in the form of the two *babas* (holy men) who were hired to exorcise Pinky. The first is a *tantrik* who sets up his portable altar with the traditional items most commonly found in both Hindu and Taoist magic: a *kapala* (a "skull bowl" used for sacred liquids or powders), a human skull (which is used to focus a spell or communicate with a god), candles, a knife, a trident (*trishul*), fruit (such as a lemon, which is a powerful weapon against evil in the Hindu religion), and holy scripture. His use of a "soul jar" to draw the evil entity from Pinky and capture the *khooni panja* is not dissimilar to the clay ghost jars seen in Taiwanese supernatural cinema; for example, the evil Taoist wizard's collection of such ceramic containers from Tso Nam Lee's **KUNG FU WONDER CHILD** (*Ling huan tong zi*, 1986 [see my "Taiwanese Fantasy Flicks" article in *Monster!* #7]). There is even the odd dualistic nature of the ghost/corpse/live human with its corporal and non-corporal coexistence. That is an entity which is rarely addressed in Western horror films, but is taken for granted in most Asian fright flicks.

A big gripe for me when it comes to Talwar's films is their lack of a decent release. Only one of his horror films, **TERI TALASH MEIN** (1990) was ever released on DVD. The print is very good (not taken from badly transferred, beaten-up VHS/Beta source material) and the DVD comes with English subtitles. Too bad it is not a monster film, but one of those annoying "woman in white" thrillers designed as a wannabe ghost flick (a similar "Scooby-Doo" monster movie, **RAAT KE ANDHERE MAIN** [1987] is another disappointment). The currently available VCD for **KHOONI PANJA** is from TNT Video, but the print they used for their disc has seen better days, and it would have helped if the compression used in processing the digital video wasn't so buggy. The VCD sleeve art that TNT's creative staff came up with is a mishmash of images from the film (i.e., the monster and the possessed girl), and right smack in the middle is the scaly face of Ray Harryhausen's hideous Medusa from **CLASH OF THE TITANS** (1980, USA), of all things! This sort of outright theft is not that uncommon within the Indian horror community. Heck, as I pointed out earlier, Talwar isn't innocent of this either. This is not the first time I've seen the Medusa incorporated into the artwork for Indian VCDs or DVDs. In fact, I'm actually considering an article on this rampant plagiarism within Indian cinema…but that will have to wait for a future issue of *Weng's Chop*.

So, will this film ever turn up on DVD unedited/uncut? Talwar has told me that unfortunately there is no plan whatsoever to have any of his films released either alone or as part of any DVD set.

The decaying ghost-monster in **KHOONI PANJA** has one of the most shockingly grotesque appearances of all of Talwar's monsters. Pictured above right is the vampire from his **FRIGHT NIGHT** remake, **WOHI BHAYANAK RAAT**, and to the right is another of his "Woman in White" *churail/mohini* witch-monsters from **HATYARIN**

Apparently it has something to do with the rights ownership to his films, the original negatives not being readily available, or possibly he just doesn't want anything more to do with them. His films were given tribute in Ashim Ahluwalia's **MISS LOVELY** (2012 [reviewed in *Weng's Chop* #5]), wherein the monsters from both **KHOONI PAN-JA** and **WOHI BHAYANAK RAAT** are anachronistically featured (the film takes place in the mid-1980s, whereas both of Talwar's originate from a later date). Too bad. There is a print of the film available to watch on YouTube, but that source is from Bimbo Video. BV is a company known for releasing obscure films on really bad-quality VCD sets, and the YT upload is from one of their worst jobs ever. However, that may well be the only way most of the world can see **KHOONI PANJA** today.

CREATURE 3D
(a.k.a. **CREATURE**)

India, 2014. D: Vikram Bhatt

A real monster movie is a very rare event in Indian cinema, no matter what industry produced it. Bollywood director Vikram Bhatt is one of the new generation of horror film directors who, along with Ram Gopal Varma, has helped mold India's approach to the genre…for good or bad. Bhatt began his career in 1992, not in horror films, but rather directing crime thrillers, political actioners, and family dramas. His first horror film was the supernatural thriller **RAAZ** (2002) which was a rip-off—*er*, an "unofficial adaptation", let's say—of Robert Zemeckis' **WHAT LIES BENEATH** (2000). RAAZ was a huge blockbuster for Bhatt and helped kickstart the new Indian horror cycle along with Varma's **BHOOT** (2003). Since then Bhatt has had hits (and misses) within an assortment of genres; his horror films have included **FEAR** (2007; a flop), **1920** (2008; super-hit), **SHAAPIT** (2009; hit), **HAUNTED 3D** (2011; hit), **RAAZ 3D** (2012; super-hit), and our present title **CREATURE 3D** (2014; flop).

With **CREATURE 3D** Bhatt had high hopes of re-introducing India to the idea of monster movies. In a recent interview, he boasted (as many directors do in India) about the importance of his new film: "It [*i.e., the monster – ed.*] has the same amount of screen-time as the hero and heroine. I know for sure that when the audience sees it, they will make others see it too. If this works, we would have opened a whole new avenue for other filmmakers in India."[6] The problem was that he had no idea

Top: A trio of humans face the might of the supernatural *brahmarakshasa*. **Center:** The CG-powered threat, whose facial expressions were provided by director Vikram Bhatt, as were its funky roars. **Bottom:** Bipasha Basu, leather-clad and armed with an elephant gun, faces down the demon. Bhatt, like Talwar, relied on traditional Indian monsters for these two productions reviewed, rather than ripping-off Hollywood horrors. Granted, some liberty was taken as to the appearance of the monsters in both of their films

---

6 *http://www.hindustantimes.com/entertainment/bollywood/will-creature-3d-redefine-the-horror-genre-in-bollywood*

how to work with what was essentially your basic monster-on-the-prowl plot *circa* the 1980s and make it Indian. Bhatt introduced a uniquely Indian creature with his creation of the *brahmarakshasa*, but at the same time had he taken the time to really develop a film around the monster, then maybe **CREATURE 3D** wouldn't have tanked at the theatres. As one critic put it, "This is the type of film in which the human beings are so annoying that you are actually rooting for the creature that kills them. In fact, the creature had more personality than all of them put together."[7]

The film opens up with a scenic view of a lush Indian jungle, with a hotel snuggled in the foliage. A woman has purchased this old hotel, and is readying it for the grand opening of "Summer Hill". Ahana is a highly-stressed, pill-popping beauty (Bipasha Basu, who previously appeared in Bhatt's **RAAZ** [2002], **FOOTPATH** [2003], **AETBAAR** [2004] and **RAAZ 3D** [2012]), who has sunk all of her life's savings into her "new" hotel. The first sign of trouble is the death of a deliveryman by some mysterious beast that attacks his van. It rips though the canvas covering of the truck then breaks through the wooden floor boards and drags the screaming man to his death. That is the first sign of the monster. Hotelier Ahana's first visitors are a group of four annoying post-grads (i.e., monster fodder) out for fun. More guests are on their way for her grand opening. She has the usual problems when it comes to opening a business for the first time: faulty oven in the kitchen, a persnickety chef, financiers checking up on their investments, and hiring a handsome singer Kunal (Imran Abbas Naqvi) for the night's festivities. The last thing Ahana needed was a hungry demigod/monster crashing the party!

7 http://www.hindustantimes.com/entertainment/reviews/moview-review-by-anupama-chopra-bipasha-basu-s-creature-3d-is-foolish/article1

The next day at the local hospital, police investigators examine the severed leg of the delivery man. Could it be the work of a lion, tiger or leopard perhaps? No, something else altogether. They also encounter a group of annoyed village folks who blame a monster. *Monster?* Don't be ridiculous!

Meanwhile, back at the hotel, the first pair of annoying guests—a recently married couple there on their honeymoon—are attacked by an unknown reptilian creature. The beast is not clearly seen, but it is clearly lizard-like and larger than a man. The husband is killed and his wife is mauled and left for dead. She is thereafter discovered by the Forest Service and rushed to the hospital. Faced with some bad press, Ahana breaks down in front of Kunal, who confesses that he is in reality not a singer, but a writer looking for a story. They connect, and we get the second horrible gushy musical number by Mithoon Sharma.

Later that night the Hotel's chef is killed by the beast when he steps outside for a drink and to make a cellphone call. Back in Mumbai, the woman who was attacked blames a monster for the death of her husband. Hearing of her tale, zoology prof Professor Sadana (Mukul Dev) packs his bags and journeys to Summer Hill to help. Meanwhile, Ahana and Kunal hire a big game hunter to track down and kill the beast. He successfully bags a leopard, and everyone parties down. Just when it seems like everything is back to normal, it's time for another song (sung by Kunal) so that the two lovebirds can gaze into each other's eyes and flirt again. As soon as the song ends we finally get a good look at the monster as it attacks two more guests inside the hotel, killing both men. The beast's (rather stupid-sounding) roar can be heard throughout the establishment, and Ahana investigates, coming face-to-face with the huge reptilian creature. The monster chases her through the hotel, and Ahana barely escapes with her life when

The *brahmarakshasa* is ready to feast! For all the thrashing about there is very little gore in **CREATURE 3D** other than some bloodshed and severed limbs.

If the monster doesn't interest you, there is always the very fetching Bipasha Basu there to keep your mind off the poor effects work in the film.

the thing is distracted by a room full of tasty-looking guests. The beast attacks the guests but Anaha confronts it, and is just about to become its next course on the menu, when from out of nowhere Professor Sadana drives the monster off with a flaming torch. In the aftermath, Ahana is left with a trashed hotel and her guests flee the compound.

Sadana then sits Ahana and Kunal down and explains that he has been studying the race of monsters called *brahmarakshasa*. He calls them mutants, men who were cursed by the god Lord Bharma and transformed into beasts due to some sort of evil transgression during their lifetime. These *brahmarakshasa* (literally, "the demons of Brahma") are doomed to walk the earth forever without any hope of ever finding salvation through reincarnation. Prof. Sadana advises Ahana to simply close down the hotel and leave. It's not just a supernatural monster that is causing her problems, as her financial backers are also pressuring her to sell them her share so they can run the hotel properly. What is a girl to do? "I have no choice but to fight", is her response.

The two team-up with a pair of local Forestry Ranger roughnecks and arrange a *brahmarakshasa* hunt. The five of them are armed to the teeth—high-powered rifles loaded with bullets blessed with fig-tree ash—and have a plan. They place a human-shaped dummy filled with blood in an abandoned bus and hide out in the brush to wait for the creature. They don't have to wait for long as the monster stomps out of the forest towards the bus. One of the rangers panics and is killed outright. Our gang of monster-hunters are then forced to flee back to the hotel when the barrage of bullets they unleash at the thing has no effect on it. The next day they regroup and travel to one of the only Brahman temples in India[8] for some advice on how to handle the monster. Meanwhile, Ahana discovers that Kunal *isn't* the famous writer, but rather Karan Malhotra, the chairman of the same builder group that Ahana feels was responsible for her father's suicide. She is devastated by this revelation, and their budding love hits a rocky spot (oh, the drama!). Ahanna's life is spiraling down into a black hole: her last-hope hotel is closed, a monster remains on her property, her boyfriend is a fraud, and she's back to gobbling pills and contemplating suicide (cue another sappy vocal music track!).

Luckily for her, the son of a late *brahmarakshas*-hunter arrives on the scene and agrees to help. Together with the remaining Forestry Ranger, the hunter, Sadana and Ahana track the monster to its underground lair, which is littered with half-munched bodies. The hunter is armed with an old elephant gun and has seven magic bullets that he believes will kill this *brahmarakshas*, like his father did one decades ago. They encounter the monster, and after some bloodshed and a waste of bullets, only Ahana gets out of the grotto alive, with a gun and just three bullets left. She is rescued by Karan, who arrives and whisks her away in a jeep. In the process he sustains some monstrous scratches, and Ahana drops him off at the local hospital. It's about time for another soulful song about rebuilding their love, etc…

8 Among the few Hindu temples dedicated to Lord Brahma, situated at Pushkar in the Indian state of Rajasthan

When Karan recovers they return to the hotel together and wait for the monster to make an appearance, with Anaha lugging the huge elephant gun. The creature slithers back to the deserted hotel, and it's a battle to the death as the lady of the land, Karan and the monster tangle.

I find it fascinating that Vikram Bhatt went out of his way to rely on an Indian monster rather than a Hollywood knock-off. While **CREATURE 3D** surely wasn't the first such creature film made in the past five years: for instance, Louis Wilson's **KAALO** (2011 [reviewed in *Weng's Chop* #2]) and Narayan/Shankar's **AMBULI** (2012 [reviewed in *Monster!* #4]) had featured fearsome beasties which were based on Asian regional folklore. Bhatt has tried to get away by saying that his *brahmarakshasa* film is the first CG-rendered monster movie made in India. That's a half-truth at best, since director Kodi Ramakrishna was responsible for introducing CG as the go-to SFX for mythological/devotional/horror cinema in 1995 with **AMMORU**. There are few truly effective sequences in the present film, and this is due to Bhatt's horrible use of low-grade animation for his monster. This is pretty much SyFy Channel material! He could have instead used all the money he sunk into the animation and come up with some fine practical suits like those developed for the films **KAALO** and **AMBULI**, which were made on a fraction of **CREATURE 3D**'s budget.

I may seem like I'm bitching about **CREATURE 3D**, but I did enjoy it despite all the plot holes and the usual nebulous Indian sense of film-flow and time (so what *did* the monster do while folks travelled all over India to temples, hospitals, etc.? Sit in a banana tree and twiddle its claws waiting for them to return to the hotel?!). The film bombed, so I don't think we'll be seeing a sequel anytime soon. As much as it pains me, Bhatt should stick to the genre that makes him money: ghostly possession films.

On a final note, I find it both amusing and frustrating that Indian filmmakers are, for the most part, boastful bores. Just prior to **CREATURE 3D**'s release, Bhatt wrote an open letter to Narendra Modi, the Indian prime minister, requesting the PM to sit through a special screening of his new monster movie. This took some balls, but not a lot of brains. The letter reads as follows:

"Dear Mr. Prime Minister, in the year 1943 my grandfather, Shri Vijay Bhatt made a film by the name of **RAM RAJYA**. The unique distinction that this film had was that it was the only film that Mahatma Gandhi saw in his entire lifetime and 70 years later I, Vikram Bhatt, his grandson, am the only filmmaker to have the distinction of making a film that has its main villain entirely generated by computer graphics imagery. The film is called, **CREATURE 3D**".

Geez!

AFTERTHOUGHT: EXPLOITING YOUR LOCAL RESOURCES FOR FUN & PROFIT

Statue of *Brahmarakshas* outside of a shrine in Kerala, India. Good and evil is relative in much of Hindu religious text.

I am always happy to watch just about any horror or supernatural film from India. Sadly, for the most part, many of the new ones "borrow" elements from Hollywood productions. When that happens, facts are changed to integrate the storyline into something which the Indian audience will appreciate. So, when a film like **CREATURE 3D** comes along, I'm dying to see if it is an original product or not. The monster that appears in the film is called a *brahmarakshasa*, a Brahma Rakshasa. These demonic critters—holy men who lost their way and turned into evil entities—have appeared throughout Hindu religious literature for centuries. For **CREATURE 3D**, director Bhatt chose to have as his "star" a reptilian humanoid which is, as mentioned in the film, a supernatural *mutant* so as not to offend folks (there are temples for popular *Brahma Rakshasa* in parts of South Asia). Sure, Bhatt's film isn't the best, but at least he tried to present something new(ish) utilizing a regional evil to drive the plot of his film. The film flopped, but I hope it inspires other directors to follow Bhatt's lead. *Please.*

ANTHROPOPHAGUS

(*Antropophagus*, a.k.a. **THE GRIM REAP-ER** a.k.a. **THE BEAST** a.k.a. **MAN-EATER**)

Reviewed by Jason Cook

Italy, 1980. D: "Joe D'Amato" (Aristide Massaccesi)

Legend has it that Joe D'Amato's new project was all ready to go, with the exception of a terrible script. Joe called his long-time buddy and collaborator, George Eastman (Luigi Montefiori), to help him rewrite the story into something he could actually direct. George agreed, but as long as he could play the lead role, which was the monster in the film, and so **ANTHROPOPHAGUS** (1980) was born. In America during the golden age of VHS, many knew this film as **THE GRIM REAPER**, in a cut version released by Film Ventures International. Some gorehounds may have even had a bloodied George Eastman on their wall; it was one of four posters featured in *Gorezone* #18. When the film premiered in Italy, it had a whopping four people or so in the theater according to Eastman, who was in attendance. But in time, the film won the hearts of millions across the globe and found its fan base.

Aside from Eastman, all of the dudes in the film never went on to have much of a career, but check out the all-star female cast: Tisa Farrow is the leading lady, hot off the success of Fulci's **ZOMBIE**, which came out a year before this film. During the same year **ANTHROPOPHAGUS** came out, Farrow did **THE LAST HUNTER** (*L'ultimo cacciatore*, a.k.a. **HUNTER OF THE APOCALYPSE**) with director Antonio Margheriti and then sadly gave up acting altogether. Actually, it's not that sad; I never found her attractive anyway. Zora Kerova had a supporting role and a year later made exploitation history when she got hung by meat-hooks through her tits in Umberto Lenzi's **CANNIBAL FEROX** (a.k.a. **MAKE THEM DIE SLOWLY**). The beautiful Serena Grandi plays a pregnant woman. Unfortunately, her fake stomach and baggy clothing cover up her two biggest assets. (She has *huge* tracts of land!) You may know her from the title role of Tinto Brass's **MIRANDA** (1985, Italy), or my personal favorite, Lamberto Bava's **DELIRIUM: PHOTO OF GIOIA** (*Le foto di Gioia*, 1987, Italy).

The movie begins with a couple making their way to the beach on a Greek Island. The dude puts on some giant headphones so he can listen to his latest Italian techno mix (DJ Pluto K, in da house!). His girl strips down to her bikini and goes for a swim. A small boat catches her eye, and when she swims over to check it out, something from beneath pulls her under. We don't get to witness the carnage, just a cloud of blood in the water. We see a POV shot of the thing that killed her making its way on land. Its presence scares off one of the local beach dogs as it gets closer to its next victim. Somehow it's got a meat cleaver, and whacks the poor guy right in the head. The film then cuts to a group of tourists who have planned a boat trip. They are going to sightsee and visit multiple islands in the area. A girl named Julie (Farrow) joins them. Unexpectedly, they meet when Arnold (Bob Larson) breaks her camera, and, since Julie needs to get to an island not too far from where the group is headed, they give her a ride. Keep an eye out for a little bearded guy with a camera around his neck when everybody gets out of the cable car together. It's *Joey D.* himself, making a cameo!

While on the boat, Daniel (Mark Bodin) offers Julie a refreshing cola and strikes out in his attempt at flirting with her. Julie seems to have some chemistry with Alan (Saverio Vallone), and the two hit it off as he gives her a little lesson on navigation. The first sign of trouble arrives when Carol

Antropophagus

TISA FARROW · SAVERIO VALLONE · VANESSA STEIGER
MARGARET DONNELLY · MARK BODIN · BOB LARSON
e GEORGE EASTMAN e con ZORA KEROVA
regia di JOE D'AMATO

(Kerova) pulls out her tarot cards to give Maggie (Grandi) a reading about her unborn child. She exclaims, "...when you ask the cards about the future and the cards don't answer, it means that there is no future for the person asking". A little later, in dramatic fashion, Carol throws her cards out into the sea. When they arrive at Julie's island and dock, it doesn't take more than a few steps away from the boat before they realize something is seriously wrong. They all head into the town, except for Maggie, who stays after spraining her ankle. The vibe is weird and unsettling. The island appears deserted, so they split up to look for someone and perhaps a clue to what is going on. Alan and Julie discover that the last telegram to leave the island was a month ago. Daniel and Carol spot a woman in a window, but right after they pursue her, she seems to vanish into thin air. In the house are some corpses and a mirror with the words "GO AWAY" written on it; but these meddling kids plan to stick around 'cause it looks like they've got another mystery on their hands. Actually that's not entirely true. They do stick around, but only because a certain mutant monster has lifted the anchor to their boat, decapitated the captain and kidnapped the hottie with the bun in the oven. Believe me, this monster wants that fresh-baked bread! After it gets dark, they find a place to crash and Carol babbles out, "There's evil on this island, an evil that won't let us get away. I sense its vibrations right now, vibrations of intense horror." Yeah, and should we make a *friend* of horror? Who does she think she is, Colonel Kurtz? After Carol's chilling statements, Julie and Daniel

hear a noise and team up to see what it was. After coming up empty, they take a sigh of relief and out of nowhere, a kitten who has a full-grown cat's meow falls onto a piano, scaring the crap out of them. A moment later, a spaced-out girl covered in blood pops out and stabs Danny Boy in the back. I forgot to mention that the reason Julie wanted to go to the island was because she was meeting a French couple and took care of their blind daughter many years ago. This traumatized chick Rita, (Margaret Mazzantini) is the blind girl all grown-up, and with her family dead she joins the company of these doomed vacationers. After Rita calms down, she explains that there is an evil being who has killed everyone on the island and how her sense of smell has been keeping her alive. She can smell this beast a mile away and hide before he gets her. Daniel, who has the worst timing in the world, tries to make out with Julie right in front of Rita! (So romantic.) This, just moments after Carol wrapped up his injury and got rejected by him. Carol walks in on his attempt to play tonsil hockey with Julie and the jealousy causes her to run out into a "day for night" shot of a forest. Julie chases after her to try and smooth things over, but crazy Carol locks her in a graveyard. With the two girls gone, Rita picks up that smell of death and Mr. Anthropophagus shows up, easily taking out Danny and then biting into his flesh for a little snack.

So where the hell did this creature come from? Did he actually come from hell? *No!* The monster was once human. He was the wealthiest man on the island. His name is Claus Weltman, or at least that's the last name I heard, maybe it was Wellman. The subtitles on the Media Blasters/Shriek Show DVD say Claus Boardman, which matches the way it sounds on the Italian language track. On the Internet Movie Data Base website he's credited as Nikos Karamanlis, but how can I trust that when the leading male's name is clearly Alan and IMDB has "Andy"?! So, let's just call him Nikos Boardman. The Boardmans decided to go boating one weekend for a little fun in the sun. The boat sank, so father, mother, and son drifted on a lifeboat for God only knows how long, until dad's stomach got the best of him. He tells his wife Martha that they should eat the dead body of their son to stay alive. She throws herself onto his knife and yells, "Now you can eat me too! *Eat me*, damn you!" The crazy bastard actually ate his own family, but his hunger didn't stop there. Once he made it back to shore he then turned the whole island into an all-you-can-eat buffet. Once a handsome family man, he is now a cannibal who looks like a half-melted clown with a beard and dresses like he stole his wardrobe from the Brawny paper towel guy, sporting a flannel shirt. Somewhere in Mr. Boardman's deranged mind he knew not to eat his sister Ruth (Rubina Rey). She was the lady that they saw through the window when they first arrived. His good old sister roams around hiding all of the dead victims' bodies (leftovers...*yum!*), apparently so the authorities won't find any of the evidence, that's what it said in her half-burnt diary. As if even the fuzz could stop The Grim Reaper!

ANTHROPOPHAGUS is pretty much Joe D'Amato's first straight horror film, and it's a pretty entertaining one. It does get slightly dull here and there, but we have Marcello Giombini's score to keep our ears happy. His music ranges from crazy keyboard compositions on crack to churchy organ music and a tune that sounds like a bastardized version of the **A CLOCKWORK ORANGE** theme. The movie suffered a lot by being cut when it was on VHS, pretty much making it almost worthless for gore fans. I wasn't thrilled about the film when I first saw it in this state, but it did have a certain something that I just couldn't quite put my finger on. It got a boost in popularity and notoriety when it made Britain's "Video Nasty" list. Fans of the film who only saw the cut version can now live the dream. We can finally see George "Anthropophagus" Eastman in one of his most infamous scenes, where he rips a fetus right of Grandi's stomach and takes a bite. The movie is about as illogical as it gets, and there are plenty of plot holes. If you haven't seen it, my advice is to keep your expectations low and you'll agree that

this is a D'Amato classic and is pretty darn fun to watch. Oh, and they made a sequel but that's just "absurd", right? *Wink-wink!*

ABSURD
(*Rosso Sangue*, a.k.a. **MONSTER HUNTER** a.k.a. **HORRIBLE** a.k.a. **GRIM REAPER 2**)

Reviewed by Eric Messina

Italy, 1981. D: "Joe D'Amato" (Aristide Massaccesi)

I've seen the original **ANTHROPOPHAGUS** at least five times, and for the first couple of viewings, I passed out. Maybe it was that **CLOCKWORK ORANGE** rip-off song by Marcello Giombini that lulled me into a coma, I'm not sure.

I was apprehensive about watching this sequel, known in some circles of hell as **ZOMBI 6: MONSTER HUNTER**. There are so many pseudo-sequels created just to cash-in on the Fulci craze, or "Fulcimania" that swept the nation for a brief period in a fictional parallel universe. If anything, this film is a rip-off of Rick Rosenthal's **HALLOWEEN 2** (1981, USA), and that works to its advantage, making it a lot more fun than it should be.

This sequel has two actors I'm very fond of, ones that Skunkape (a.k.a. Jason Cook) is always

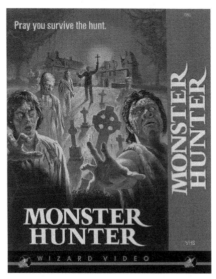

US VHS Box art for **ABSURD** with artwork by Lucio Crovato

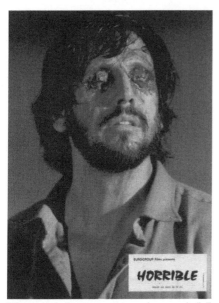

HORRIBLE

"*Mamma mia*, those are some-a spicy eye-a-balls!"

bale, a.k.a. **CANNIBAL HOLOCAUST: THE BEGINNING**, 2004, Italy]) mentions it's "absurd" that Eastman could have recuperated so fast. Don't you just *hate* when they actually say the title; at least, that's a pet peeve of mine!

There are a lot of English voice performers Italian horror fans associate with their favorite actors, like Ed Mannix (Al Cliver's voice) and a new actor I've discovered named Ted Rusoff, who dubbed the voices for characters in **CANNIBAL FEROX, RATS – NIGHT OF TERROR**, and now this.

In these straight horror films, Joe D'Amato (or "Joey D.") leaves the porn elements out, which always kind of turn my stomach anyway (unless they involve Laura Gemser, of course). Maybe his "Adult" work wasn't really cutting the mustard that month, so he figured: why not steal from John Carpenter!

They overly establish the hospital location, almost as if this is the shittiest episode of *General Hospital* or **HALLOWEEN 2**; which to me is basically a 94-minute bad episode of that show masquerading as a slasher movie.

A sergeant, who hates Greeks for some reason, encounters both opposing characters (Eastman and Purdom) and racially profiles them. Perhaps he knows that those babaghanoush eaters are bloodthirsty killers, according to this prejudiced film.

Edmund Purdom plays a Dr. Loomis-type priest who claims that he "serves God with biochemistry". He's trying to catch Mikos Stenopolis, the beastly invader (Eastman), who is basically immortal. Mikos can only be killed by destroying the brain, like one of the living dead (or pick your favorite slasher villain). He becomes more of a "Michael Myers"-style figure toward the second half and is lurking outside waiting to strike anyone that leaves the house. The bearded freak's blood keeps regenerating, and as soon as he sees Purdom's character, he grunts like he's trying to shit an atomic brick! The first victim of the Greek bruiser's wrath is a poor nurse who gets a surgical instrument plunged beneath her ears and out through her skull.

I have to mention how stupid it is to have another Greek character who escaped from a mysterious island and not have it be Nikos Karamanlis (who Eastman played during the first film in this supposed "sequel")! I mean—yeah, semantics and everything—but why have the same actors, director and similar premise and then go and invent a totally new threat? That aspect reminds me of how in **TERMINATOR 2**, Schwarzenegger returned as a slightly different model, playing a totally un-

busting my chops about. They are Edmund Purdom and George Eastman (or Luigi Montefiori). I first saw Purdom in Juan Piquer Simón's **PIECES** (*Mil gritos tiene la noche*, 1982, Spain) as the maniacal campus dean responsible for all the carnage (and I'm still not sure how an elderly frail guy was capable of such brute force)! Both *Grim Reaper* sequels were put on the hypocritical "Video Nasty" list.

The man-eating protagonist of Greek origin, played and written by Eastman, would never make it back to the States and terrorize suburbia (or would he)? The original gut-scarfing, fetus-devouring landmark to me is cinematic narcolepsy, and the sole reason I stayed away from this sequel for so long. To me the original doesn't age well with repeated viewings, like you'd imagine.

This time around, it's all about the next "Grim Reaper" or *Anthropophagus*—which is just a fancy word for cannibal. Italian superstud George Eastman hops a gated fence that tears open his stomach contents…*Ooof*, that smarts! Then he winds up in the hospital as surgeons do their best to patch him up, but they have no idea who they are messing with, because he wakes up midway through sedation. I'm no scholar or medical professional, but this could mean that he's (1) either an indestructible freak or (2) on PCP!

One of the doctors (whose dubbed voice sounds like Bob Manson, the sinister reporter from Bruno Mattei's **CANNIBAL WORLD** [*Mondo canni-*

related cyborg from the first film. I highly doubt that James Cameron saw this film and pitched the idea to anyone, but you never know, and he's definitely a hack in my book.

For the sake of argument, just pretend it's the same dude from the first movie and let it slide, because there's no race of Greek atomic cyborgs waiting to appear in **ANTHROPOPHAGUS 3**! I have to admit though, **ABSURD** is much better than the first film!

Michele Soavi ("Mr. **DEMONS** himself") makes a cameo appearance as an unlucky motorist, whose "good Samaritan intentions" become his early grave. That guy has been through the Italian sausage-ringer numerous times as victim or leader, and it's pretty impressive that he's still around, working in film. There's a scene where a little kid named Willie freaks out that his babysitter is watching a soap opera which has Mark "Warty Balls" Shannon and Laura Gemser, Jr. (both actors from D'Amato's **PORNO HOLOCAUST** [see *Weng's Chop* #6]). Had I been drinking any liquids, I would have immediately done a spit-take on my computer! There's a terrible babysitter that taunts Willy the kid about the "Boogie man who's coming to get him". For some reason they dress up the boy to look like Little Orphan Annie—how humiliating! The babysitter gets smacked on the top of her head by brain-squashing hammer; I guess she kinda deserved it. There's also a nasty band-saw lobotomy that gave me the heebie-jeebies!

At one point the music sounds exactly like "killing 2 parrots with one cracker" from the **CANNIBAL FEROX** soundtrack. Carlo Maria Cordio, who did the score for this, has quite an (un)impressive background, and worked on **TROLL 2, SONNY BOY**, Lenzi's **EATEN ALIVE!** and **CANNIBAL FEROX**. So the music is not entirely stolen, since the guy was in the recording booth helping Budy Maglione (or Robert Donati) out.

There are some scenes where the film quality is grainy (that's what I get for watching this on YouTube)! One really gruesome part involves the monster shoving a girl (played by an unrecognizable Annie Belle) into the oven, which singes her hair off and she then retaliates by stabbing him in the neck a bunch of times. The creature gets really pissed-off when a bedridden girl in the house pops out his eyeballs with a sharp drafting compass. The sightless maniac lumbering around looking for the one responsible and Purdom swooping in to help at the last minute is pretty much ripped off from **HALLOWEEN**. That being said, it's a good **HALLOWEEN** rip-off, and I enjoyed this movie for all its flaws, because it was not as boring as the first film.

Italian genre auteurs steal from everyone in the book, but are able to get away with it because they do it seamlessly. This film had some deceitful looking video boxes, like the one for **MONSTER HUNTER** (see pic, p.17), which is sort of a cross-breeding of Ulli Lommel's **THE BOOGEYMAN** (or **BOGEYMAN** in the UK) and **BURIAL GROUND**. There's a blue video sleeve for **AB-SURD**, with a blood-drenched battle axe—which reminds me of He-Man—and another that resembles a **STAR WARS** rip-off. Maybe someone was tricked into renting it, believing it was a family-friendly Ewok turd. Check it out if you like your hummus extra-pulpy with chunks of brain matter!

NOTE: In Eric's **VOODOO BLACK EXORCIST** review in *M!* #9, I mistakenly assumed he meant **THEY MIGHT BE GIANTS** the movie, rather than the band of the same name; hence, while proofing his piece I caused a bit of an error. My bad! [SF]

CASTLE OF BLOOD
(*Danza macabra*)

Reviewed by Matt Bradshaw

Italy/France, 1964. D: "Anthony M. Dawson" (Antonio Margheriti) and "Gordon Wilson, Jr." (Sergio Corbucci)

The fact that this is an atmospheric, castle-bound creepfest from the Golden Age of Italian Horror would have been enough to get me in the theatre door. The knowledge that it stars Barbara Steele would have had me down front with the jumbo tub of popcorn, but no soda. Answering nature's call during a Barbara Steele flick? *I think not!*

Colorful metaphors aside, I first discovered **CASTLE OF BLOOD** on VHS from Sinister

Georges Rivière as hero Alan Foster in **CASTLE OF BLOOD**

Barbara Steele as the alluring undead vixen of CASTLE OF BLOOD

Cinema in those dark pre-digital days. I was surprised to learn the very same fullscreen print is the one Amazon has available for streaming, complete with Sinister Cinema's "SC" bug in the bottom right of the screen. It's hard to scoff at that $1.99 rental price, but if you can see beyond the instant gratification of streaming, the widescreen version is available on Synapse Films' DVD, which you can rent from Netflix. The DVD features a nice crisp widescreen picture and also reincorporates several scenes cut out for the original U.S. release, which can easily be spotted, as the dialogue suddenly switches to French with English subtitles.

The opening credits claim the film is based on Edgar Allan Poe's "Danse Macabre". Before you send a terse email to your high school English teacher for leaving this gem out of the Poe unit you did back in tenth grade, be advised that Poe never wrote such a tale. Perhaps inspired by Roger

Corman's Poe films of the time, someone probably decided the author's name carried marketable recognition factor.

Alan Foster (Georges Rivière who also appeared with Christopher Lee in Margheriti's **HORROR CASTLE** [*La vergine di Norimberga*, a.k.a. **THE VIRGIN OF NUREMBERG**, 1963, Italy/France]) is 19th Century journalism's answer to annoying paparazzi. When American author Edgar Allan Poe (Silvano Tranquilli who previously shared the screen with Steele in **THE HORRIBLE DR. HICHCOCK** [*L'orribile segreto del Dr. Hichcock*, a.k.a. **THE TERROR OF DR. HICHCOCK**, 1962, Italy]) visits London but refuses our hero's request for an interview, Foster tracks him to a bar called The Four Devils. After some light verbal sparring over the finality of death and Poe's extraordinary claim that his stories are all based on fact, the author's drinking companion, Sir Thomas Blackwood (Umberto Raho of **THE LAST MAN ON EARTH** [*L'ultimo uomo della Terra*, 1964, Italy/USA], **THE BIRD WITH THE CRYSTAL PLUMAGE** [*L'uccello dalle piume di cristallo*, 1970, Italy/W. Germany] and **BARON BLOOD** [*Gli orrori del castello di Norimberga*, 1972, Italy/W. Germany]) bets that Foster can't spend a night in the Blackwood family castle. Blackwood makes this same wager every year, but no one has ever managed to survive the night; in fact, the young couple who took the challenge the previous year are currently buried in the family graveyard. Foster takes the bet, not being a believer in the supernatural, and Poe and Blackwood are soon dropping him off at the remote family estate.

This creepy **CASTLE OF BLOOD** cadaver may have been the work of the film's co-director Margheriti, who was a seasoned SFX man

Mexican lobby card

After some nicely creepy explorations by candlelight of the dusty cobweb-strewn castle, including some eerie harpsichord music and some ghostly dancers, Foster learns he is not alone. Sir Thomas's sister Elizabeth (Barbara Steele) resides in the castle, and she tells Foster that every year on this night her brother sends her someone to keep her company. Our hero can probably be forgiven for not realizing Elizabeth's spectral nature, as her lips (among other things) soon prove to be quite tangible, but the romantic snuggle—during which he notices she has no heartbeat—should really have been a wakeup call. I don't want to give too much more away, but there's plenty of infidelity, murder, and nefarious goings-on to keep the viewer satisfied.

Shot in English but dubbed after the fact, the slightly out-of-synch audio adds an enjoyable otherwordly vibe, and Foster and Elizabeth fall in love with such blinding speed it almost gives the feel of a tragic fairytale. The black-and-white cinematography, the score, and some good old-fashioned ghostly sound effects combine for an atmospheric little scare flick. One would think that a film called **CASTLE OF BLOOD** would benefit from a really cool-looking exterior shot of said castle...but it never happens. This seems like a missed opportunity for a matte artist.

And of course there is Barbara Steele. She is wonderful as usual, which makes it all the more unfortunate when she disappears for a long stretch in the middle of the movie. The lady has an amazing screen presence, and an unusual type of beauty that can best be described as slightly sinister. The arch in those eyebrows could hook a man's very soul! While my top two Steele films remain **BLACK SUNDAY** (*La maschera del demonio*, 1960, Italy) and aforementioned **THE HORRIBLE DR. HICHCOCK, CASTLE OF BLOOD** acquits itself nicely with the bronze.

HALLOWEEN III: SEASON OF THE WITCH

Reviewed by John Harrison

USA, 1982. D: Tommy Lee Wallace

Ad-line: *"The night no one comes home..."*

After Rick Rosenthal's **HALLOWEEN II** (1981, USA) failed to live up to the critical acclaim and box-office takings of John Carpenter's original 1978 genre-defining slasher film, producers and financiers felt that the saga of ghostly stalker Michael Myers had been exhausted, yet were keen to continue to capitalize on the name and

21

"HALLOWEEN III"

"HALLOWEEN III"

Mad masketeer Dan O'Herlihy (top), and Tom Atkins with Stacey Nelkin (above) in a pair of U.S. lobby stills for **H3: SOTW**

legacy—not to mention a substantial core fan-base—which **HALLOWEEN** had so successfully established. To that end, it was decided in 1982 that the best way to keep the franchise fresh and moving forward was to approach the series as an anthology, releasing a different and completely self-contained film every October, each one unrelated yet still presented under the *Halloween* umbrella. Unfortunately, while this idea was an intriguing and potentially promising one, the resulting first film in this proposed anthology series, **HALLOWEEN III: SEASON OF THE WITCH**, died such a swift death at the box-office, and was met with almost universal disapproval by fans at the time of its release, that the producers and money men quickly abandoned their original plans, bringing Michael Myers back for a series of increasingly generic sequels, beginning with **HALLOWEEN 4: THE RETURN OF MICHAEL MYERS** in 1988.

While I've always admired the style and iconography of the original **HALLOWEEN**, **HALLOWEEN III** has always been my favourite instalment in the long-running series (ten entries so far, including Rob Zombie's 2007 remake

and its sequel). Written and directed by Tommy Lee Wallace (his debut feature, after working in various capacities on John Carpenter's early films), **HALLOWEEN III** eschews the stalk & slash formula of the first two movies and opts for a much darker tale of witchcraft and the occult, with a dash of science fiction added to the blend. The result is a film that combines the grisliness of early '80s horror with the paranoia of classic 1950s sci-fi. There's also the undeniable feel of an Americanized, updated Quatermass adventure, something not overly surprising considering Quatermass creator Nigel Kneale had a go at an early draft of the screenplay (Wallace estimates that approximately 60% of the completed screenplay contains elements or ideas from Kneale's initial draft).

HALLOWEEN III opens strongly in a mysterious fashion which quickly draws you into its plot, and lets the viewer know straight away that this is going to be a very different *Halloween* film indeed. As John Carpenter's moody synth score fills the soundtrack, a lone figure races along a deserted highway late at night. Clutching a latex Halloween mask in the shape of a jack o' lantern, the middle-aged man appears exhausted as he is pursued by two mysterious and emotionless figures dressed in business suits, who are clearly out to do the man some harm. Dispatching one of his pursuers by crushing him between two cars in a closed lot and giving the other the slip, the man eventually collapses into the arms of a gas station attendant, who drops the rambling stranger off at the nearest hospital.

Refusing to let go of his mask and mumbling, "They're going to kill us. They're going to kill us all", the man, who turns out to be small-town shop owner Harry Grimbridge, is placed into the care of Dan Challis (Tom Atkins), a divorced on-call doctor who is going through some tension with his ex-wife, primarily over the repeated broken promises he makes regarding time spent with his two young children. He doesn't remain a patient for long, however, as the man in the business suit whom Grimbridge had earlier given the slip turns up at the hospital in the middle of the night, killing the man by tearing out the bridge of his nose with his fingers, before dousing himself with petrol in the hospital parking lot and turning himself and his vehicle into a funeral pyre, as Challis and several other hospital staff watch on in horror.

Drawn into the violent mystery, Challis and Grimbridge's daughter Ellie (Stacey Nelkin) decide to investigate the strange death further, their leads taking them to the small Californian town of Santa

Mira, where Grimbridge had recently been seen putting in an order for Halloween masks from Silver Shamrock Novelties, a thriving business owned by mysterious Irishman Conal Cochran (Dan O'Herlihy), who appears to have his run of the town, and is constantly surrounded by a brigade of expressionless men dressed in similar suits to the ones who pursued Grimbridge. Posing as a couple, Challis and Ellie check themselves into a small roadside motel in Santa Mira, along with several other wholesale customers of Silver Shamrock, one of whom mysteriously dies in the middle of the night, when she curiously scratches away at a Silver Shamrock logo that has fallen off one of her masks, causing a laser to shoot out and hit her in the mouth, melting her face away. Challis and Ellie grow increasingly suspicious of Cochran and Silver Shamrock, and become convinced that her father lost his life after stumbling upon something at the factory.

Finding himself cut off from communicating with anyone outside of the town, Challis infiltrates the Silver Shamrock factory after Ellie is kidnapped by the men in suits. While snooping around, Challis is horrified to discover that these men are actually androids created by Cochran, who has concocted a fiendish plot to bring All Hallow's Eve back to its dark and serious origins. This he plans to achieve by implanting a secret electronic chip, infused with a tiny fragment of stolen rock from Stonehenge, into every Silver Shamrock logo on their three popular Halloween masks: The Green Witch, The Skull and Pumpkin Head. When a special planned Silver Shamrock commercial airs nationwide on Halloween night, a signal in the transmission will activate the chip in every mask, killing the wearer in an extremely gruesome fashion, and unleashing a swarm of deadly insects and snakes to kill everyone else around them (the sequence where Cochran gives Challis a glimpse at his plan, by locking an obnoxious couple and their mask-wearing little kid Buddy in a room and playing the commercial for them, is still an effectively chilling and disturbing moment, and shows a level of violence towards children that is rarely seen in studio movies today). As the clock counts down, Challis faces a desperate race against time to try to rescue Ellie, defeat Cochrane and his android assassins, and convince the television networks to pull the Silver Shamrock commercial off the air before the whole of America is plunged into a primordial nightmare.

There is so much to admire about **HALLOWEEN III**, making its somewhat neglected status amongst fans even more disappointing (though attitudes towards the film have certainly changed for the positive in recent years). Writer/director Wallace shows a sure and confident hand with the material, and there's an effective atmosphere of menace and dread that pervades throughout much of it, not to mention an astonishingly dour and downbeat ending, the type that films like Don Siegel's **INVASION OF THE BODY SNATCHERS** (1955, USA) would love to have had at the time, were studios not so insistent on optimistic conclusions. Siegel's classic clearly exerts a strong influence on **HALLOWEEN III**, sharing a similar tone of distrust and paranoia, and even the emotionless animatronic robots can be seen as the film's version of **BODY SNATCHERS'** pod people. And of course, **INVASION OF THE**

If megalomaniacal mask manufacturer Conal Cochran has his way, there shall be *real* monsters a-prowl on this Halloween night!

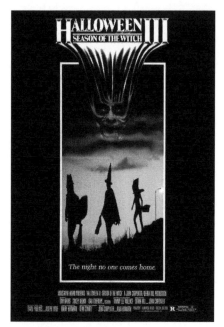

The night no one comes home.

BODY SNATCHERS also took place in a fictional town called Santa Mira. Reference is also made to the original HALLOWEEN, with a television commercial announcing a special Halloween airing of "the immortal classic".

Filmed for the most part in the small town of Loleta, California (population 783 as of 2010), HALLOWEEN III looks terrific through the lens of cinematographer Dean Cundey, and as previously mentioned the score by John Carpenter and Alan Howarth is a triumph of experimental synth tones and dark melodies which perfectly complements the film's atmosphere and sci-fi undertones. There's also the memorable Silver Shamrock jingle, composed by Wallace and set to the tune of "London Bridge is Falling Down" ("*Eight more days to Halloween, Halloween...*") which plays incessantly throughout the movie, on both television and radio. It's catchy, annoying, cheesy and creepy all at the same time.

Tom Atkins, coming off a string of Hollywood genre hits like THE FOG (1980), ESCAPE FROM NEW YORK (1981) and CREEPSHOW (1982), makes for an unconventional but solid male lead, likeable despite being something of a deadbeat to his ex-wife and kids, flicking them—and his promises—aside in order to take off on an adventure with the much younger Ellie (and it isn't long before the pair are sharing a little motel room sack time, initiated at the suggestion of Ellie). Stacey Nelkin is cute and likeable enough as Ellie, but her role is a

rather undemanding and underwritten one (Nelkin, who dated Woody Allen when she was 17 and he was 42, has claimed that Allen's 1979 classic MANHATTAN was based on their relationship. She had mostly retired from acting by the mid-1990s, and now works as a "relationship expert"). Veteran Irish actor Dan O'Herlihy (THE LAST STARFIGHTER, ROBOCOP) is tremendously effective in his role as Conal Cochran, a sense of maliciousness and evil never far below his smiling, friendly exterior. With a cheeky glint of childlike mischievousness in his eyes, O'Herlihy's appearance certainly adds an extra veneer of class to the production.

At the time of its release, HALLOWEEN III inspired the usual tie-in memorabilia: soundtrack LP, paperback novelization (by Dennis Etchison, writing as Jack Martin) and a *Fangoria* cover feature. But it did also boast a pretty cool and bold marketing concept, by having the famed Don Post Studios mass producing the three masks which they had designed for the film, and making them commercially available to fans (*Fangoria* ran full-page color ads offering them for sale, at prices ranging from $31.95 for The Skull to $49.95 for The Green Witch. Pumpkin Head was in the middle at $39.95). The Don Post Studios were also featured in the film itself, doubling for the rooms of the Silver Shamrock factory in which the masks were being produced. *[See John's Don Post article on p.69]*

In 2012, to celebrate its 30th anniversary, Shout! Factory did HALLOWEEN III justice by releasing a great "Silver Shamrock" special edition on Blu-ray and DVD, with a wealth of supplementary features including two audio commentaries, a nice making-of featurette, trailers and TV/radio spots, an episode of *Horror's Hallowed Grounds* which revisits the locations of the film with director Wallace, and more. Customized action figures have also been produced in recent years, and the original Don Post masks were reissued by Trick or Treat Studios (after the Post Studios closed its doors in 2012).

HALLOWEEN III: SEASON OF THE WITCH may not be a monster movie in the true sense of the word, though Conal Cochrane can certainly be viewed as something of a human monster. But it's one of the best movies made both for and about Halloween, a true gem of early '80s American genre cinema, and along with Tobe Hooper's initially much-maligned TEXAS CHAINSAW MASSACRE 2 (1986, USA), a nice reminder of a period when filmmakers were willing to be creative and take chances with horror movie sequels. It's just a pity that it took many fans so long to start appreciating their efforts.

WALKING DEAD & SHE-SERPENTS: HAMMER'S "CORNISH HORRORS"

by Troy Howarth

Before the bottom fell out, Hammer Films enjoyed a lengthy period of prosperity. In 1965, producer Anthony Nelson-Keys (1911-1985) lighted upon the idea of cutting corners even further in order to maximize profits. Nelson-Keys figured that if they were to produce two films back-to-back on the same sets, utilizing many of the same production personnel, they could make an additional savings—then have a couple readymade double bills by pairing each film off with another film being produced the same way. Thus, they put **DRACULA–PRINCE OF DARKNESS** and **RASPUTIN – THE MAD MONK** into production in 1965, then green-lit a pair of films which would become known among fans as "the Cornish horrors" early the following year: **THE PLAGUE OF THE ZOMBIES** and **THE REPTILE**. **DRACULA–PRINCE OF DARKNESS** and **THE PLAGUE OF THE ZOMBIES** would go out as co-features in January of 1966, with **RASPUTIN–THE MAD MONK** and **THE REPTILE** following a few months later. Given that Hammer's star attraction, Christopher Lee, provided star power as Dracula and Rasputin, there was less need for a major name for the US market in the two Cornish features. As such, the Cornish films would be seen as the B film of each double bill—but in the estimation of many fans and critics, they outclassed the main features rather handily. (That being said, I must confess a preference for **DRACULA–PRINCE OF DARKNESS** among the four films; but that is another discussion for another review.)

Nelson-Keys entrusted **PLAGUE** and **THE REPTILE** to a reliable journeyman whose association with the company stretched back to the early 1950s. John Gilling (1912-1984) made a name for himself as a screenwriter and script doctor before making the transition to directing. He helmed the Bela Lugosi comedy **OLD MOTHER RILEY MEETS THE VAMPIRE** (a.k.a. **VAMPIRE OVER LONDON**, 1952) and the superior Burke and Hare horror-drama **THE FLESH AND THE FIENDS** (a.k.a. **MANIA**, 1959) before making his debut for Hammer with the Hammer-in-everything-but-name **THE SHADOW OF THE CAT** (1961). Its status as an "official" Hammer title remains contentious, but a viewing of the film should be enough to remove all doubt: it was filmed at Hammer's base of Bray Studios with the usual technical personnel (cinematographer Arthur Grant [1915-1972], production

ASSOCIATED BRITISH-PATHE LIMITED presents A HAMMER FILM PRODUCTION

THE PLAGUE OF THE ZOMBIES 'X'

starring

ANDRE DIANE JOHN
MORELL CLARE CARSON

also starring

ALEX **DAVION**

JACQUELINE **PEARCE**

BROOK **WILLIAMS**

Screenplay by
PETER BRYAN

Produced by
ANTHONY NELSON KEYS

Directed by
JOHN GILLING

TECHNICOLOR •

RELEASED THROUGH
WARNER PATHE

Here's a slightly misleading piece of artwork that appeared in British newspapers at the time of the film's initial release. While the zombies may have been shambling brutes, they in no way resembled Universal Studios' classic image of the Frankenstein monster

designer Bernard Robinson [1912-1970], etc.) very much in place. He then directed the stylish swashbucklers **THE PIRATES OF BLOOD RIVER** (1962) and **THE SCARLET BLADE** (a.k.a. **THE CRIMSON BLADE**, 1963), and provided a rich and imaginative screenplay for **THE GORGON**. When that film emerged in 1964, Gilling was furious to see that much of his script had been junked by producer Anthony Hinds (1922-2013) and director Terence Fisher (1904-1980), with the former having rewritten large chunks of it and jettisoning the rest. Gilling, never known as an especially warm and cuddly sort of person, never forgave Hinds for doing it or Fisher for allowing it to happen. Thus, when the time came for Gilling to direct his first proper Gothic horrors for the company, he did so with a chip on his shoulder and a burning desire for a little sweet revenge.

THE PLAGUE OF THE ZOMBIES went into production first, and it remains the more popular of

the two pictures; indeed, for many, it remains one of Hammer's most memorable concoctions. The story tells of a corrupt Squire (John Carson) who becomes involved with voodoo while spending time in Africa. He brings the ancient religion back to Cornwall and uses it to enslave the local populace, killing off strapping young men and using voodoo to control their bodies after death. This proves beneficial for furnishing cheap labor for his tin mine, but a meddling Professor (André Morell [1909-1978]) gets wind of what is going down and decides to put a stop to it...

Beginning with its opening voodoo ceremony and working its way through to a nightmarish "rising from the dead" sequence which so impressed director Martin Scorsese that he used a clip of it in his terrifying episode of *Amazing Stories* ("Mirror, Mirror"), there is very little wrong with **THE PLAGUE OF THE ZOMBIES**. If we must address the negatives, let us do so quickly and succinctly: the climax shows a poverty of imagination, as we are treated to yet another fiery blaze; and of budget, as the otherwise superb makeup effects by Roy Ashton (1909-1995) are undercut by some very unconvincing fireproof mask-work. In addition to this misstep, the film is also burdened with a couple of stilted and unconvincing performances courtesy of Brooke Williams (as the local village doctor whose wife succumbs to the "plague") and Diane Clare (as Morell's naïve daughter). But *that's it* for the negative, so let's move on to the positive!

Hammer films are rightly celebrated for their use of actors like Christopher Lee and Peter Cushing (1913-1994), but these two stars were not the only stand-outs in their stable of acting talent. **PLAGUE** showcases André Morell and John Carson in the usual Cushing (hero) and Lee (villain) roles, and they acquit themselves admirably. The script allows them a few witty jabs as they square off against each other, and both actors have the benefit of tremendous charisma and screen presence in addition to obvious acting talent. It's to be regretted that Hammer did not capitalize on them by utilizing their services more often: Morell's association with the company goes back to the surgical melodrama **STOLEN FACE** (1952), and would include memorable turns in **THE HOUND OF THE BASKERVILLES** (1958, as Dr. Watson), **THE CAMP ON BLOOD ISLAND** (1958), **CASH ON DEMAND** (1960) and aforementioned **THE SHADOW OF THE CAT**, as well as less memorable appearances in **SHE** (1964), **THE MUMMY'S SHROUD** (1966) and **THE VENGEANCE OF SHE** (1967), after which the company stopped reaching out to him; Carson would go on to appear in **TASTE THE BLOOD OF DRACULA** (1969) and **CAPTAIN KRONOS—**

VAMPIRE HUNTER (1972), as well as an episode ("Guardian of the Abyss") of *The Hammer House of Horror* TV series in 1980. Both actors absolutely nail their respective characters and give the film a solidity which helps to anchor it in reality. Among the supporting cast, Jacqueline Pearce is a standout as Brooke Williams' sickly wife; she doesn't have a great deal to do, really, but she does it well and would be rewarded with a more substantial role in THE REPTILE. Hammer stalwart Michael Ripper (1913-2000) is also on hand as a constable—*of course!*—and he gives his usual polished, endearing performance.

The outstanding music score by James Bernard (1925-2001) helps to set the right atmosphere, while Bernard Robinson's sets are convincing without being unduly expansive; Hammer's penny-pinching was starting to become a little obvious around this time, but Robinson's genius for stretching these pennies as far as they could go would remain an asset to the company until his death in 1970. As for Gilling, he may have been a cantankerous pain in the ass on set, but he sure knew how to do his job. THE PLAGUE OF THE ZOMBIES is stylish and well-paced, with rich atmosphere and excellent performances. It is most definitely his finest Gothic for the company, and one of the best horror films they would ever produce.

THE REPTILE deals with a doctor of theology (Noel Willman [1918-1988]) who meddles in

British poster

Eastern religion and incurs the wrath of an Indian sect. His daughter Anna (Jacqueline Pearce) is afflicted with a most unusual curse, which results in her transforming into a ghastly reptile woman whenever her emotions are aroused. Hoping to keep her safe, he moves her to a small Cornish village and takes up the life of a recluse, but inevitably the secret will not stay hidden for long…

The amazing—and hugely influential—"rising of the dead" sequence from **THE PLAGUE OF THE ZOMBIES**

THE REPTILE allowed Gilling to revisit elements of his screenplay for **THE GORGON**. Appropriately enough, the screenplay was the work of Anthony Hinds (under his usual pseudonym of John Elder), thus providing Gilling with a chance to apply a bit of Karma as he saw it. He radically reworked the script and wasted little opportunity in bad-mouthing the original version in interviews whenever the topic came up. Just precisely how Gilling modified the story is a matter for conjecture, but what he came up with certainly works well enough and is thematically rich. The film continues the dialogue on the specter of colonialism looming over rarified English country life from **THE PLAGUE OF THE ZOMBIES**, but if it has a problem it's that not enough really happens. Whereas **THE PLAGUE OF THE ZOMBIES**

was sure-footed and exciting, **THE REPTILE** proceeds in fits and spurts; when it works, it works very well indeed, but when it drags, it really drags. The end result is uneven, but still compelling.

Noel Willman and Marne Maitland (1920-1991) play the roles one could easily picture being performed by Cushing and Lee. Willman had already top-lined **THE KISS OF THE VAMPIRE** (1962), in which he played the droll and deadpan leader of the vampire cult, and he would go on to appear as a wizened soothsayer in **THE VENGEANCE OF SHE**, which was hardly a career highlight for anybody involved other than leading lady Olinka Berova (*née* Olga Schoberová, Brad Harris' wife). Willman's restraint pays off with a wonderful portrait of a man coming apart at the seams, even as he desperately tries to keep it together. He doesn't play up for audience sympathy in the way that Cushing might have done, and his chilliness makes the character more interesting, especially when he finally caves under pressure at the end. Marne Maitland had already impressed as a corrupt Indian aristocrat in **THE STRANGLERS OF BOMBAY** (1959) and did what he could underneath unconvincing "Chinese" makeups in aforementioned **THE CAMP ON BLOOD ISLAND** and **THE TERROR OF THE TONGS** (1961). Maitland's courtly, civilized manner makes him a soft-spoken, insidious sort of villain. Some of the film's best moments come when he needles Willman's character or presides over Anna as she begins to transform. As for Pearce, she fulfills the promise of **PLAGUE** with a more properly developed characterization in this film. Anna

Top & Above: Panels from the comics adaptation of **THE REPTILE**—scripted by Steve Moore and penciled by Brian Lewis—which ran in the UK's *Hammer's House of Horror* magazine (#19, April 1978; published by Top Sellers Ltd. of London)

is an innocent who is suffering due to her father's transgressions, making the film yet another exploration of the "sins of the fathers" theme so prominent in so many Hammer horrors. She is sympathetic as she struggles to understand what is happening to her and is properly frightening when she finally transforms. Michael Ripper is on hand yet again, this time with one of his most substantial and affecting performances, as a kindly tavern keeper—*naturally!*—who helps unravel the mystery. Craggy-faced Australian actor Ray Barrett (Werner Herzog's **WHERE THE GREEN ANTS DREAM** [a.k.a. *Wo die grünen Ameisen träumen*, 1984]) and pretty and spunky Jennifer Daniel (**THE KISS OF THE VAMPIRE**) make for an unusually matched pair of lovers, and they have genuine chemistry. Only John Laurie's (1897-1980) over-the-top portrayal of the village loon, Mad Peter, seems a bit overdone.

The reptile makeup is hotly debated among fans, of course. There's little doubt that the actual design work is first class, but something appears to have gone wrong in the execution. No doubt Roy Ashton simply didn't have adequate time and resources to do the job properly, but he does what he can under the circumstances and the makeup actually comes off better in the film than it does in the many unforgiving frame grabs and publicity stills which have been reproduced down through the years. Gilling sensibly does not dwell on the horrific visage for long, and the shadowy lighting helps to keep the seams invisible. Truth be told, the film's several big shock sequences are among the best in any of Hammer's horror films, with nasty tactile details like the foaming of the victims' mouths and their blackening skin providing an extra frisson, as well.

Both **THE PLAGUE OF THE ZOMBIES** and **THE REPTILE** were released theatrically in the US by Twentieth Century-Fox and both would become late-night TV staples in the 1980s. It took a while for them to crop up on home video, but Anchor Bay rectified that in the late-1990s when they issued both films to VHS and laser disc. The widescreen, uncut transfers looked pretty sweet at the time, but time has not been kind to either transfer, especially with regards to the upgrades that were done for DVD. For their debut on Blu-ray, Optimum have gone back and done up brand new HD transfers; the results are mouth-watering! **PLAGUE** remains one of the best-looking Hammer HD transfers to date: the print is in very good shape, detail is very sharp throughout, and those vivid primary colors (just look at those red hunting jackets!) are wonderfully rendered. Optimum have also adjusted the opening of the film to reflect the original continuity: a decision was made late in the day to bump the credits to approximately the mid-point of the pre-credit sequence, creating a jarring jump-cut in the music and

Jacqueline Pearce's fearsome were-snake was cover girl on the September 1966 ish of Warren Publishing's *FM* spin-off mag, *Monster World;* released some months after the film received its U.S. release in April '66

some dodgy continuity on screen; Optimum have reinstated the titles to where they were originally intended to be, and the result is smoother and more satisfying. **THE REPTILE** starts off looking a little rough, with its pre-credit sequence looking a bit soft and the opening credits looking especially worn, but fear not: after that, the quality of the transfer improves exponentially. The remainder of the film is much more detailed and aesthetically pleasing than any other version presented on home video to date, revealing some nice use of gel lighting in some of the cavern sequences. Both films are presented in their original mono sound mix and the soundtracks are clean and clear, with ample presence afforded to their thundering music scores. Both titles are also afforded newly-produced featurettes, which include comments from actors like John Carson and Hammer scholars like Jonathan Rigby. They are well-produced and edited featurettes, relying more on comments from the interviewees than on padding things out with endless clips, and they both provide an ample understanding of the production of the films under discussion. Trailers and stills galleries are also included. The only downside for US viewers is that these are Region B releases, but really—if you are a fan of Hammer horror in particular, this is as good a reason as any to upgrade to a region-free Blu-ray player. You'll be glad you did.

Louis Paul's

CREATURE FEATURES MAd MONSTERS FROM THE TUBE

For this issue I've decided to take a look at some now nearly forgotten made-for-television movies of the 'Seventies. They all feature a monster, and in my opinion, they are above-average tales of terror.

Growing up in the 'Sixties and 'Seventies, television was what we watched after school, in the evening with family, and—if you were lucky enough to have your own set in your bedroom—what you watched late, late at night. While the occasional obscurities and low-budget fun filled our eyeballs during the late hours, Saturday mornings and nights...there was other monster fun to be had.

For fans of the macabre, Dan Curtis' Dark Shadows (1966-71) was our beacon of light airing live on ABC-TV during the late weekday afternoons. When I got home from school, I barely had time to prepare to enjoy what Barnabas Collins and company were up to in that day's episode. Sure, even at a young age I could tell that the acting was all over the place, sometimes names were mispronounced, or lines forgotten, and at other times sets moved and things fell from papier mâché walls. But, damn! This show featured vampires, ghosts, eerie orchestral music, creepy kids and more. Although Christopher Lee was, is, and forever will remain "King of the Vampires" for his portrayals of Count Dracula in so many films and appearances, Jonathan Frid's Barnabas Collins was my go-to guy for American vampires for a long time...until Robert Quarry came on the scene with Count Yorga. Besides Dark Shadows, I was content with reruns of The Twilight Zone (1959-64), Alfred Hitchcock Presents (1955-62), Thriller (1960-62, with host Boris Karloff), The Outer Limits (1964-65), and so on, with Rod Serling's Night Gallery (1969-73) ushering us into the '70s. But, if I recall correctly, those previously mentioned television series were different, with each week—or night, if they were already in rerun syndication hell—a new cast, a new story, something dramatic, something horrific, something with a hint of fantasy, something lightly comical...but always with a hint of the macabre.

If there was another program like Dark Shadows on U.S. television in the '60s where much of the same cast could be seen on a daily basis in a horror-oriented program (and, yes folks, I think DS

Jonathan Frid as Barnabas Collins in Dan Curtis' supernatural soap opera, *Dark Shadows*

was and remains one of the very few horror-themed soap operas of its time), I don't think I've seen it. Sitcoms like The Addams Family and The Munsters (both 1964-66) were entertaining in their own way, but for the purposes of this piece, I'm not including them. The only show that was jarring on a continual basis, and even more so, was Quinn Martin's The Invaders (1967-68). Shown on ABC television on Sunday evenings, this two-season series was co-created by genre fave Larry Cohen for television producer Martin, who was looking to replace his successful man-on-the-run show The Fugitive with something new and different...and yet familiar. Cohen's take on that four-year hit starring David Janssen was inspired by two short-lived series of his own (Branded [1965-66] and Coronet Blue [1967]), as well as Don Siegel's **INVASION OF THE BODY SNATCHERS** (1955, USA), and others. Decidedly downbeat at times, the sci-fi paranoia tale The Invaders most likely alienated adult viewers acclimated to the police procedural dramas Martin produced like aforementioned The Fugitive *(1963-67) and* The F.B.I. *(1965-74). Not as fondly recalled today as is the product from much more prolific '60s-'70s TV wunderkind Aaron Spelling, Martin's shows seem to have a heavy air about them. Heck, I still recall the booming voice intoning "A Quinn Martin Production!" with much ballyhoo at the start of every episode of* The Invaders *and* The F.B.I.[1]

In its short run, The Invaders *racked-up an amazing 43 episodes, and these were generally filled with a high level of paranoia and conspiracy theories about aliens, alien invasions and the possible likelihood of government agencies working with said aliens for some unspecified reasons (I would bet that Chris Carter was partially influenced by this show when he was penning some of the finest* X-Files *episodes tackling similar material). During the entire run of the series, Roy Thinnes played the stoic "David Vincent" in a manner that was guarded, and unemotional.*

What brings us full circle here is that Roy Thinnes plays "David Norliss" in Dan Curtis' THE NOR-

---

1 Other Quinn Martin TV productions of note are *The Untouchables* (1959-63, with Robert Stack), the WW2-themed *Twelve O'Clock High* (1964–67, with Frank Overton), *Dan August* (1970-71, with Burt Reynolds), *Banyon* (1971-73, with George Peppard), *Cannon* (1971-76, with William Conrad), *The Streets of San Francisco* (1972-77, with Karl Malden and Michael Douglas), and *Barnaby Jones* (1973-80, with Buddy Ebsen).

LISS TAPES*, a strange, atmospheric chiller produced and directed by the man behind* Dark Shadows *and the* Night Stalker *films.*

THE NORLISS TAPES

USA, 1973. D: Dan Curtis
*Wr: William F. Nolan, Fred Mustard Stewart
S: Roy Thinnes, Angie Dickinson, Vonetta McGee, Don Porter, Hurd Hatfield, Nicolas Dimitri*

When the 1972 television movie **THE NIGHT STALKER** (whose shooting title had been "THE KOLCHAK TAPES") became a runaway hit for the ABC television network—for years it was noted as the most-watched television program—and its creator Dan Curtis was working on the follow-up film a year later, rival TV network NBC wanted Curtis to consider developing a project for them. While the production of **THE NIGHT STRANGLER** was ongoing and talks were turning towards a third *Night Stalker* film or even a television series, which Curtis was considering, he chose instead to work on **THE NORLISS TAPES**. We assume today that this was intended as a pilot for a series, but possibly the dark subject matter, or execution—or something *else* entirely—led to this becoming an odd side-note to television horror history.

David Norliss (Thinnes) appears to be a successful writer of books that peel back the layers of truth

Roy Thinnes as David Norliss and Angie Dickinson as Ellen Cort discover the grotesque golem-in-progress during **THE NORLISS TAPES**

about the occult and paranormal. What exactly the subjects of those books were are left to the viewer's interpretation, but Sanford Evans (Don Porter), his agent, editor, publisher and longtime friend of Norliss is concerned—after a large advance and one year later—that his latest project is taking so long. Norliss is one of those journalists who seem to dig deep through layers of muck in order to find the truth, and his latest project, writing about California's '70s scene of mediums and psychics, is a way to expose them as leftover '60s radicals and acid heads. But when a disoriented Norliss calls Sanford one day saying he's really disturbed by something he's uncovered, he implores him that they should meet ASAP. That's when things begin to get eerie…

Sanford drives out to a house perched near a cliff that overlooks the San Francisco bay. It's raining ferociously when he finds a sliding glass door left open. Once inside, he finds much of the house in disarray. Bottles of bourbon and whiskey are lying about, and there's the sense that something bad happened here. On a table lies a typewritten page with an ominous note. Intended as the beginning of a book that never got finished, it reads, "Chapter One – I shall try to put this down, even though I now know I may never finish this. It all began…" There's also a tape recorder and a batch of numbered audiocassette tapes nearby. Sanford puts number one into the tape recorder, lights a cigarette, sits back…and so begins our tale of the supernatural. David Norliss' weak, fatigued voice is heard on the tape, listing events of his investigation into the supernatural and encountering a fake medium and ghosts…and then he speaks about Ellen Cort (Dickinson).

Ms. Cort is a sister of Norliss' friend who seeks his help because she's heard of his dealings with the supernatural. It seems that Ellen's late husband, a paralyzed sculptor named Jim (Nicolas Dimitri), has returned from the dead as a blue/grey skin-toned ghoul and is up to something in his old work space. One night, upon hearing strange sounds Ellen went to investigate and her now seemingly seven-foot-tall, ghoulish man-ape of a dead husband snarls like a beast at her, the family dog lunges but is swept aside, after which Ellen pumps a few bullets from a shotgun into her husband's already dead body…and then calmly walks out into the night air, stricken with fear. The police of course found nothing but the body of the dog, and blood that they presume to be that of the deceased animal. They figure that the woman shot the dog by accident in a moment of fright. Ellen explains that her late husband Jim was a victim of dementia as well as being wheelchair-ridden, but was in a constant search for a cure…and then they met Madame Jeckiel (Vonetta McGee).

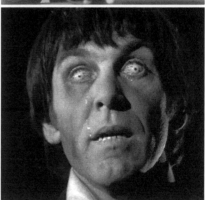

Top: Thinnes as Norliss, in a posed publicity photo. **Above:** Seasoned Hollywood stuntman/actor Nick Dimitri as **THE NORLISS TAPES'** reanimated sculptor-run-amuck, James Raymond Cort

It appears that the sexy caramel Ms. Jeckiel is also an artist, and one who dabbles in the occult. Somehow, before his death, Ellen's husband became the bearer of the ring of Osiris, (apparently) an Egyptian God of the Dead. He believed that he could cheat death by wearing it…and was buried with it. Well, before one can say "Let's make a *Night Stalker* rip-off with a similar but different leading investigative character", David Norliss is running around San Francisco and often getting in the way of a police investigation into a series of murders of local women. It's got to be tough when the local sheriff is played by Claude "I don't take any shit!" Akins

Dimitri as Cort exhorts his finished statue to assume an unnatural and unholy life (see below pic)...

(who had likewise played another representative of law enforcement in the original *Stalker* movie).

Along the way to finding out why Jim Court's re-animated corpse is killing women at night, Norliss encounters a mysterious art gallery owner played by Hurd Hatfield, and more women in colorful filmy gowns (if this wasn't a made-for-TV movie, I'm sure nipples would be seen thrusting through all these flimsy fabrics!). Of course the previously mentioned "Ring of Osiris" figures into the resurrection, and by the finale we actually get to see why Jim's cold-blooded killer monster corpse is sculpting in the studio: it's a *golem*! Actually, it's supposed to be Sargoth, an Egyptian demon...but it

...and Sargoth is reborn to walk the Earth anew!

looks mighty like a cross between a muscular interpretation of Satan and the Golem from that German silent film of the past. Crazed undead grunting Jim is using the blood of his victims mixed with clay to bring his creation to life.

In the caves below the Cort estate—yes, for some reason there is a labyrinth of cavernous catacombs right below the grounds—Norliss and Ellen discover a few bodies, including Madame Jeckiel's. Thinking fast that the removal of the ring will end the reign of tower, Norliss paints a circle around the sculpture and hides in the studio with Ellen. When the reanimated husband returns and finishes his art (cue heavy rain and lightning), the demon statue begins to come to life...but I would be spoiling all if I gave away the ending here.

The movie's coda comes with the tape ending and Norliss' editor Sanford lighting another cigarette and reaching for another cassette...perhaps another story that may lead to finding out whatever happened to David Norris.

Effectively directed without tongue in cheek, Dan Curtis did a fine job on **THE NORLISS TAPES**. After the end of *The Invaders* in '68, Roy Thinnes starred in the superior Gerry Anderson science fiction film **JOURNEY TO THE FAR SIDE OF THE SUN** (a.k.a. **DOPPELGÄNGER**, 1969, UK), and was memorable in the dark supernatural Western tele-movie **BLACK NOON** (1971, USA). I'm sure there was much thought brought to **NORLISS** being a pilot for an eventual series, but Thinnes' casual, cold line readings and bland interpretation of the hero doesn't exactly warm the viewer into siding with the character (unlike Darren McGavin's scandal-hounding news reporter Carl Kolchak in **THE NIGHT STALKER** and its spinoff series). It didn't help that Curtis and teleplay writer William F. Nolan—yes, the guy who wrote *Logan's Run* (1967)!—crafted some mush-mouthed narration for Thinnes to glibly intone:

"As I headed for the Cort estate along the seventeen-mile drive, acres of lush Cyprus and tall pine loomed over me. The ocean below bellowed and roared, smashing into the coastline, spilling white foam along the sand. There's no doubt this rugged peninsular country could give the French Riviera tough competition. But on this afternoon, my mind really wasn't on the scenery. I kept thinking about the girl who had been murdered the night before, trying to tie what I knew about her into the story Ellen told me. I had a gut hunch the two were connected. How, I don't know. But I was going to have to find out!"

Angie Dickinson plays a variation of the older-sexy-woman-in-peril role that we've all seen

Darren McGavin (1922-2006) as '70s pop culture icon Carl Kolchak strikes a typical pose in **THE NIGHT STALKER**. For all his smartassery and obnoxiousness, we couldn't help but love the guy!

countless times before, and despite the fact that we've seen her kick ass both before—e.g., **THE KILLERS** (1964, USA) and **POINT BLANK** (1967, USA)—and after (the tough *Police Woman* teleseries [1974-78, USA]) she really doesn't impress much here, and the way she's photographed

In classic vampire fashion, Barry Atwater as the predatory, ferocious bloodsucker János Skorzeny recoils from Kolchak's silver cross. In much the same way as Christopher Lee's Dracula characterizations were, Atwater's non-speaking performance relied on body language and sheer energetic physicality to convey Skorzeny's bestial ferocity

by DP Ben Colman there are many times when she's just plain unrecognizable. The supporting cast is fine, with the stunning Vonetta McGee stealing every scene she's in, however brief, in the middle of her many appearances in a batch of Blaxploitation films (**BLACULA** [1972, USA] and **SHAFT IN AFRICA** [1973, USA], among others), but she's not provided much to do via the tailored script calling for a sensuous, mysterious woman of the occult. Ultimately, **THE NORLISS TAPES** is a movie that is enjoyable, but not much better than I was hoping after having not seen it for decades. It's an occasionally spooky entertainment, with the best moments coming from Nick Dimitri as the killer undead husband. **NORLISS TAPES** appeared in 2006 on Starz/Anchor Bay DVD, but that is long out-of-print; however, Netflix happens to have it in stock, and that's where I got my review copy (sans any extras *[Not that AB's original DVD had any either! – ed]*).

THE NIGHT STALKER

USA, 1972. D: John Llewellyn Moxey
Wr: Richard Matheson, based on a story by Jeff Rice
S: Darren McGavin, Simon Oakland, Carol Lynley, Barry Atwater

The 1970s sure were a sleazy time to be alive, and **THE NIGHT STALKER** (whose original script was entitled "The Kolchak Papers"; the film's working title was "THE KOLCHAK TAPES") embodies that well with its opening scene. Disheveled news reporter Carl Kolchak lies on a bed in a sleazy motel, dictating notes into an even-then-archaic tape recorder. We hear his weary but self-important voice noting how this book that he is thinking of writing is about a serious of unusual murders in Las Vegas, and about the cover-up resulting in none of the truth leaking out into the real world. In a *noir*-ish *policier* fashion, we see glam girls in go-go boots being attacked, and their lifeless bodies discovered the next day. Ever an aging, fading newshound (with a trademark porkpie hat and white seersucker suit) seeking one last moment of glory, Carl Kolchak—whom we assume has seen much better days, but now bides his time working for a lesser newspaper—uses the police scanner in his car so he can turn up around the same time that the corpses are discovered. Flashing away with his instamatic camera, Kolchak's interrogation of any witnesses or family members is impersonal, impolite, bordering on the idiotic. There's barely a glint in McGavin's eyes that betrays any remorse at all. Carl Kolchak thinks he's found a news story of note when women are brutally killed by some powerful sinister

Second and third pics from top: McGavin as Kolchak and Carol Lynley as his GF Gail peruse a tome about the occult in **THE NIGHT STALKER**. **Above:** Atwater as Skorzeny, the film's always-hungry, ever-on-the-prowl undead menace

figure. When he learns that the bodies have been drained of blood, he becomes a little more somber and starts investigating deeper, much to the chagrin of the local police department and politicians. After our mysterious killer raids the blood bank of a local hospital and outwits a number of police cars chasing him down, Kolchak irritates everyone at a news conference the next day by suggesting that the killer may be a vampire. In short effect, Kolchak is banned from appearing at any crimes scenes and told to stay out of the way of the authorities.

Possibly Kolchak seeks a redemption of sorts— if he can just get his news story printed. When dozens of police officers are thrown around like stuffed animals while they try to capture the killer and Kolchak is there to witness it, he then begins to think that maybe he's in a bit over his head. Even old friend and FBI agent Bernie (a restrained Ralph Meeker) wants less to do with him. Kolchak's long-suffering editor Tony Vincenzo (Oakland) does all he can to keep the reporter from inflating his already bothersome ulcer, and Kolchak's sometime girlfriend Gail (Lynley) is worried when he suggests that she may help lure the killer into the open.

When further investigations reveal that our monster is in fact a Romanian nobleman named János Skorzeny (Atwater), who according to the files is at least seventy years old but appears and moves like a man with a true age much younger than that, Kolchak begins to believe his own vampire theories.

A showdown in the lair of Skorzeny makes for an eerie, well-edited finale as we find our sweaty, rumpled newsman holding a puny pistol in one hand and a cross in the other. The monster, having been downed by a fuselage of gunfire—the police were apparently loading silver bullets in

their guns—Kolchak barely escapes the aftermath as he is threatened with manslaughter charges or worse if he prints anything about the killer or what transpired that night. Run out of town, he and Vincenzo are holing up in a sleazy motel. Which brings us back to the beginning of the film, with Carl Kolchak speaking into a microphone trying his best to get his story down, possibly also aware that it may never be printed ("Judge for yourself its believability and then try to tell yourself, wherever you may be, it couldn't happen here").

Paced with an electric energy and acted by a game cast, the movie fails to disappoint, even after so many years have passed. About the only negative thing I can say about the film is how irritating Robert Cobert's score is to me. Heavy on jazzy horns and strings, it really feels like he's trying his best to distance himself and his score from the church organ lullabies that fueled much of his work on *Dark Shadows*.

Aired on American television for the first time on January 11, 1972, **THE NIGHT STALKER** took the world by storm. Television audiences who didn't venture into theaters to see that there was a mighty big change in the kinds of films playing there were in for a shock when violence was brought into their homes in such a fashion. Having been fed reality via news footage of the Vietnam War, maybe the filmmakers thought it was time to make a sort of *cinéma vérité* horror film for the masses. Dan Curtis produced the movie, but didn't direct it. After many years working on *Dark Shadows* (1966-71), he lightly stepped away from the soap opera when he produced the unusual Canadian/American television version of the Robert Louis Stevenson classic known as **THE STRANGE CASE OF DR. JEKYLL AND MR. HYDE** in 1968, with Jack Palance in the title roles. His first fea-

Above right: John Carradine puts in a cameo as a grouchy, free speech-quashing authority figure named Llewellyn Crossbinder in **THE NIGHT STRANGLER**

ture films as a director were **THE HOUSE OF DARK SHADOWS** (1970, USA) and its follow-up, **NIGHT OF DARK SHADOWS** (1971, USA). Possibly burned by the mixed reception to both—**HOUSE** was more than likely too violent and sexy for the soap opera crowd who beloved the show, and **NIGHT** was an uneven ghost film said to be a victim of studio tampering which was sold to audiences as a lurid sex thriller with occult overtones via a ludicrously odd marketing campaign and misleading trailer—he handed the direction chores to the prolific journeyman John Llewellyn Moxey. Noted for working on many British cult favorites like *The Avengers* (1961-69), *The Saint* (1962-69), and *The Champions* (1968-69), Moxey went to the U.S. and built a solid career working on the likes of *Mission: Impossible* (1966-73), *Mannix* (1967-75), and *Kung Fu* (1972-75). In my opinion, the best work he ever did as a director was **HORROR HOTEL** (a.k.a. **CITY OF THE DEAD** [1960, UK]) and **THE NIGHT STALKER**. Darren McGavin was an incredibly prolific actor who it seems made appearances on just about every American television series of note throughout the '60s and '70s. He was just turning 50 when the role of Carl Kolchak came along, and McGavin took to it with immense joy. He appeared in the sequel and the short-lived television series, as well. In his twilight years, McGavin made several appearances in *The X-Files* (1993-2002), a show influenced by the *Night Stalker* films and series.

T⫸E NI⫸⫸T STRAN⫸LER

USA, 1973. D: Dan Curtis
Wr: Richard Matheson
S: Darren McGavin, Simon Oakland, Jo Ann Pflug, Scott Brady, Wally Cox, Richard Anderson

"This is the story behind the most incredible series of murders to ever occur in the city of Seattle, Washington. You never read about them in your local newspapers or heard about them on your local radio or television station. Why? Because the facts were watered down, torn apart, and reassembled...in a word, falsified."

It's a year after the events of the previous film, and Carl Kolchak (McGavin) and Vincenzo (Oakland) are now working for a newspaper in Seattle as reporter and editor respectively. Echoes of "some problems" that happened in Las Vegas have kept Kolchak relegated to working on minor stories, and often Vincenzo has to put him on a short leash, lest he start investigating news items that might appear a little too ghoulish.

Before long, a series of murders are committed and young women are the victims. Could Kolchak be facing another vampire-killer? Much to Vincenzo's chagrin, Kolchak begins investigating and finds some similarities between the murders in Vegas and those here in Seattle. The Police too, are well aware of Kolchak's antagonizing the authorities on the Vegas case and are not tolerating any interference from him. So off he goes on his own, only to uncover another baffling theory behind the identity of the killer who may not be a vampire, but someone who has lived for hundreds of years (the film's original working title was "THE TIME KILLER"). This murderer kills women for a specific reason at certain times of the year, every few years... before disappearing, only to resurface and do it all over again. His victims are exotic dancers and prostitutes: people who will not be missed or cared about. It turns out that one Dr. Malcolm (Anderson, soon to be seen as Oscar Goldman on *The Six Million Dollar Man* [1974-78, USA]) is a Civil War physician who has defeated the aging process by removing certain bodily fluids from his victims—along with their blood—to make a serum that will keep him perpetually middle-aged. Malcolm hides out in the ruins of Seattle's "Underground City", which makes for a nice location for the telemovie's finale.

As in **THE NIGHT STALKER**, Kolchak, Vincenzo, and the former's belly-dancing girlfriend (Pflug) are told to leave Seattle and to never return. We're in Kolchak's car as he announces to his companions (and we the viewers) that they're heading to another major city, this time on the east coast, where presumably other adventures await.

With Robert Cobert's quasi-Lalo Schifrin music blaring out of the soundtrack ushering us back into the game, we welcome Carl Kolchak and reluctant sidekick Tony Vincenzo back for another tale of the macabre. Kolchak's girlfriend in the previous film (Carol Lynley) is absent here, and replaced by equally vapid flesh-and-blood package Ms. Pflug (who would have quite a "career" in the '70s by appearing on a variety of game shows as a contestant: *Match Game*, anyone?).

Sometimes it feels like the tongue is more in the cheek than the previous Kolchak adventure, as there's a whole lot of familiar genre faces in cameo parts (John Carradine, Al Lewis, Margaret Rutherford), and perennial *Hollywood Squares* figure Wally Cox tries valiantly in a sort of dramatic role. The mystery is good enough in this film to keep you entertained, but compared to Barry Atwater's acrobatic and powerful vampire in the first film, Richard Anderson just seems menacing; psychotic, yes, but the animal blood-lust danger that one felt with Atwater's primal performance—even if a lot of it should be credited to the stunt people who doubled him—seems to be missing here. But, rather than with Dr. Malcolm's long-winded reveal to Kolchak about his immortality and need for serum at any cost, I was more entranced with Kolchak's visit to Seattle's "Underground City" (actually sets on the 20th Century-Fox lot, but it really does exist, and you can learn more at *http://www.undergroundtour. com/about/index.html*).

As before, McGavin and Simon Oakland seem like a perfect fit for one another, their verbal sparring more welcome than irritating this time out. I think if these two actors were put together in a revival of Neil Simon's *The Odd Couple* it would have been fun. While not often recalled with the admiration given to **THE NIGHT STALKER**, **THE NIGHT STRANGLER** is a fine sequel nonetheless.

"THE NIGHT KILLERS" was planned as the

Down in Seattle's eerie underground city, Kolchak encounters Richard Anderson as Dr. Richard Malcolm, an unnaturally-sustained serial killer who maintains his eternal youth via syphoning off human bodily fluids. That second picture from the bottom reveals what happens if he misses his dosage of "juice"! Below that is the "Stop Press" news headline which never makes it to newsstands for the simple reason that the authorities pull the plug on the story

third film in the series, but ABC decided to not exercise that option, and by then Dan Curtis moved on to producing and directing **THE NORLISS TAPES** (itself a sort of more sober variation of the Kolchak stories).[2] Darren McGavin was approached by Universal Studios to star as Carl Kolchak in a television series. Neither ABC nor Dan Curtis were directly involved in the 1974-75 series *Kolchak: The Night Stalker*. It lasted only one-and-a-half seasons before cancellation. *Night Stalker*, a poorly-conceived re-revival of the Kolchak character and stories, was aired by ABC in 2005 (with Stuart Townsend as Carl Kolchak). It aired a mere ten episodes before being cancelled.

THE NIGHT STALKER and **THE NIGHT STRANGLER** were made available as a double-sided DVD released by MGM in 2004. Both prints used appear to be the non-U.S. theatrical versions, with the former featuring some four minutes of footage not seen previously Stateside, and the latter containing over nine minutes of extra scenes.

2 Dan Curtis would go on to direct the well-regarded TV movie **TRILOGY OF TERROR** (1975, USA), the theatrical feature **BURNT OFFERINGS** (1976, USA/Italy), another made-for-TV feature called **CURSE OF THE BLACK WIDOW** (1977, USA), and **DRACULA** (1973, UK), which received both TV airings and was also released theatrically in some markets; as well as the SOV tele-movie **THE STRANGE CASE OF DR. JEKYLL AND MR. HYDE** (1968, Canada/USA) and the ill-fated 1991 small screen reboot of *Dark Shadows* (1966-71, USA).

Darren McGavin stars.

TERROR
OF THE
WERE-KITTIES!

Part two

by **Steve Fenton**

Last issue I covered a handful of "were-kitty" movies which originated here in the Western Hemisphere. But, comparatively speaking, even though cats play a sizeable role in our occidental mythology and superstitions—as virtually everywhere else on the planet where such species are either indigenous or have otherwise been introduced and/or domesticated—movies involving feline-based monsters aren't really all that common in the West. In fact, although I only dealt specifically with a mere four of them in *Monster!* #9, that constituted a pretty sizeable proportion of the grand total. Although there are many western movies which showcase the "supernatural" qualities of domestic housecats (most typically black ones, natch; typically of the non-shapeshifting variety), the number of films incorporating all-out monstrous moggy-things is relatively small. In fact, other than for that quartet I reviewed last ish, I'd be hard-pressed to come up with any more titles off the top of my head. However, while in the West cat-monster movies are about as rare as

hens' teeth or tits on a bull, there are a much more substantial number to be found which originated in the Far East. Hence, for this ish, we head way, way out to the exotic wilds of the Orient, which is a far more fertile breeding ground indeed for both folklore and motion pictures (etc.) involving such supernatural or otherwise otherworldly creatures derived from the *Felidae* family. Below follows the first instalment of what I hope shall develop into a regular (if erratically-published) *M!* series: namely, coverage of "were-kitty" cinema of primarily Asian descent; and in this our bumper tenth issue I shall be starting with a pair of ultra-obscure Malaysian movies on the general theme—one little-known, but still extant; the other well-known in certain quarters, but now "lost"—as well as showcasing one very well-known Japanese movie also involving fantastical feline fiends, in addition to providing some further backstory on the *bakeneko* and *kaibyō* myths and movies of Japan, too. I'm also covering one killer kitty-critter flick of Hong Kong origin.

A wonderfully spooky image from **GHOST-CAT'S MYSTERIOUS SHAMISEN** (1938)

Above: Original Japanese posters for [left] **GHOST-CAT OF THE CURSED WALL** (1958), and [right] **GHOST-CAT OF OUMA CROSSING** (1954), with Tako Irie as the *kaibyō* on that latter poster

KURONEKO

(藪の中の黒猫 / *Yabu no naka no kuroneko*, a.k.a. **THE BLACK CAT**)

Japan, 1968. D: Kaneto Shindō

An English translation of some hype from the original Japanese trailer: *"Is She Demon or Ghost? Human...or Cat? Hungry...Baring the Fangs of Vengeance...Two Female Cats..."*

In Japanese mythology, the *bakeneko* (化け猫, "changing cat") is just one of the many supernatural creatures to be found in the teeming *yōkai* (妖怪, "phantom") pantheon. Among their many and varied abilities (which seem to vary from region to region in Japan), the *bakeneko* might speak in human language, accurse or possess human beings, or even shapeshift into them themselves, often (if not necessarily always) with sinister motives. Regional tales tell of cats that, after being cruelly killed by humans, transformed into *bakeneko* for the purposes of avenging themselves on their human if inhumane killers, typically via some horrible malediction. Sprung from similar folktales, numerous Japanese horror movies over the years have featured fearsome feline spirits and demons (variations of these occur in other parts of Asia, too). I'm not exactly sure what the precise distinction—if any—is between the *bakeneko* and *kaibyō* (怪猫, "ghost-cat") subgenres of *kaidan* (怪談, "weird tales"), but if they are technically considered different species of supernatural animals, they do typically share some highly similar and often interchangeable traits (e.g., a taste for human blood).

Shōzō Makino's silent era short *San'nō no bakeneko* (山王化猫, 1914) was one of the earliest films on the theme to be made in Japan, and numerous other pre-sound era examples were produced during the 'Teens and 'Twenties. During the 'Thirties, actress Sumiko Suzuki (1904-1985) became a popular portrayer of "ghost-cat" women in local films, including Shichinosuke Oshimoto's **GHOST-CAT OF GOJUSAN-TSUGI** (怪猫五十三次 / *Kaibyō gojūsan-tsugi*) and Kiyohiko Ushihara's **GHOST-CAT'S MYSTERIOUS SHAMISEN** (怪猫謎の三味線 / *Kaibyō nazo no shamisen*, both 1938). Ryohei Arai (1901-1980), a now largely forgotten filmmaker who made some notable entries in the genre during the 'Fifties, had directed an early "talkie" example in the fertile and enduring *bakeneko/kaibyō* genre, entitled **SPIRIT OF THE CAT** (*Shinrei jakuneko*, 1940).

In the following decade, Arai made the moody and at times manic B&W *kaidan* GHOST OF SAGA MANSION (怪談佐賀屋敷 / *Kaidan Saga yashiki*, 1953), which featured a mottled white-and-tan cat that takes the form of a woman (frequent so-called "*bakeneko* actress" Takako Irie [1911-1995], giving a truly creepy, over-the-top performance in wild, *kabuki*-style greasepaint makeup). During one crazed sequence, her "hackles" (i.e., bangs) rise to rather evoke cat's ears pricking up and she attacks a man by scratching his eye with her fingernails/claws. Like a cat playing with a ball of yarn, she then pulls him to her on a magical invisible string in order to administer the fatal jugular-bite, that latter activity much in the same way as was later seen in our present title **KURONEKO** (neck-biting and said "invisible string" ability were also staple ingredients of other films of this type). One agile and energetic demoness for sure, Irie springs about cat-like while eluding some samurai, diving through a paper wall and even crawling upside-down on the ceiling at one point (albeit c/o of a simple inverted camera shot). Also in '53, Arai made **GHOST-CAT OF ARIMA PALACE** (怪猫有馬御殿 / *Kaibyō Arima goten*), which utilized some similar themes and once again featured Irie doing her patented cat-demoness routine, and the actress returned to the genre the following year for Bin Kado's **GHOST CAT OF THE OKAZA-KI UPHEAVAL** (怪猫岡崎騒動英題 / *Kaibyō Okazaki sōdō*, a.k.a. **TERRIBLE GHOST-CAT OF OKAZAKI**, 1954), as well as Katsuhiko Tasaka's **GHOST-CAT OF YONAKI SWAMP** (*Kaibyō Yonaki numa*, a.k.a. **NECROMANCY**, 1957); these three films, all made by different directors, formed an Irie *kaibyō* trilogy. She appeared in at least two other *kaibyō kaidan-eiga*, both for director Bin Kado: namely **GHOST-CAT OF OUMA CROSSING** (怪猫逢魔ヶ辻 / *Kaibyō Oumagatsuji*, a.k.a. **CAT MONSTER OF OUMA CROSSING**, 1954) and **GHOST-CAT OF GOJUSAN-TSUGI** (怪猫五十三次 / *Kaibyō gojūsan-tsugi*, a.k.a. **CAT-GHOST OF THE FIF-TY-THREE STATIONS**, 1956).

In much the same vein, Nobuo Nakagawa's atmosphere-saturated period haunted house tale **BLACK CAT MANSION** (亡霊怪猫屋敷 / *Bōrei kaibyō yashiki*, a.k.a. **THE MANSION OF THE GHOST-CAT**, 1958) told the terrifying tale of another blood-drinking *bakeneko* (this time one possessed by the restless spirits of innocent people murdered by samurai), which assumes the form of a white-haired feline hag who eats raw (i.e., live) koi—see also this ish's Hong Kong horror **EVIL CAT** (凶猫 / *Xiong mao*, 1987)—and laps blood from a saucer like cream during the furtherance of

Top: Eureka!'s Blu-ray. **Above:** Takako Irie administers the catnip to a victim's throat in **GHOST-CAT OF THE OKA-ZAKI UPHEAVAL** (1954), one of the actress' numerous "specialized" roles in *kaibyō-eiga*

A creepy moment from
**THE GHOST-CAT
CURSED POND** (1968)

its supernatural vendetta. Featuring future "Zatōi-chi, The Blind Samurai" Shintarō Katsu in one of his earliest film roles, Kenji Misumi's **GHOST-CAT OF THE CURSED WALL** (怪猫呪いの壁 / *Kaibyō noroi no kabe*, a.k.a. **THE GHOST-CAT CURSED WALL**, 1958) also featured a ghostly cat-woman who can scale the sides of buildings with her furry, clawed hand-paws and who chews the throats out of deserving recipients, once again exacting supernatural vengeance against wrongdoings committed by immoral mortals on the earthly plane. Yoshihiro Ishikawa's **THE GHOST-CAT OF OTAMA POND** (怪奇幻影傑作撰 怪猫 お玉が池 / *Kaibyō Otama-ga-ike*, 1960) was one of the earliest entries of the '60s, and same director Ishikawa's **THE GHOST-CAT CURSED POND** (*Kaibyō nori no numa*, a.k.a. **BAKENEKO: A VENGEFUL SPIRIT**, 1968) was yet another such film made the same year as the present film under review. Which brings us to **KURONEKO**…

No stranger to supernatural shockers, its writer-di-rector Shindō (1912-2012) also wrote and direct-ed the gloomy, grim, at times brutal and chilling B&W *kaidan* **ONIBABA** (鬼婆, "*Demon Woman*", a.k.a. **THE HOLE**, 1964, Japan), with which **KURONEKO** shares a few rudimentary if notable textual similarities, not to mention the same lead actress. The literal translation of the present film's original Japanese title is "*The Black Cat from the Grove*" (at least one Japanese scholar has point-ed out the title's possible allusion to "*Yabu no naka / In a Grove*" [藪の中, a.k.a. "In a Bamboo Grove", 1922], the famous short story penned by Ryūnosuke Akutagawa [1892-1927] which pro-vided partial inspiration for Kurosawa's masterful **RASHŌMON** [羅生門, 1950, Japan]). As well as being a *jidai-geki/chanbara* period piece, the genre-spanning hybrid **KURONEKO**—which style-wise one online critic described perhaps somewhat too facilely if with the best of intentions as "Mario Bava by way of Akira Kurosawa"—is also a gothic ghost story in the classic *kaidan* mold, concerning evils committed on Earth duly facing

Things get freaky in **GHOST-CAT OF THE CURSED WALL** (1958)

dire retribution from beyond the very grave itself. In time of war sometime during the Heian period (794-1185 AD) of Japan's history, at her isolated country cottage a mother named Yone (Nobuko Otowa [1925-1994], who also played the even more cynical and world-weary mother in **ONIBA-BA**) and her daughter-in-law Shige (Kiwako Taichi [1943-1992]) are jointly raped and murdered by a ragtag passing band of bedraggled, battle-weary foot soldiers, who torch the house before leaving (symbolizing the off-handedly casual nature of their crimes, one of the men horks and gobs nonchalantly as they depart, acting as though rapine and murder are merely part of a day's work for them). The opening atrocities are dispensed with swiftly, almost cursorily, with nothing of a graphic nature being shown. In this manner, the seeds of the scenario are sown and the scene is set. Perhaps indicating some sort of supernatural intervention in their fate, the fact that the two women's home becomes their blazing funeral pyre thanks to the soldiers' act of arson makes it rather startling that after the building has been reduced to charred, smoldering wreckage all around them, their supine

corpses lying amidst the ashes and carbonized lumber remain relatively unscathed by the flames, other than for a few burns. Intensifying the perception that dark supernatural forces are involved, a softly mewling black cat—which it is later implied may be the family pet—happens upon the corpses as they lie in silent repose side by side. As per a common trope of the *kaibyō* genre, it then proceeds to lap blood from their wounds in a quietly ominous manner which seems to imply that other things besides simply slaking its thirst are motivating the creature…as indeed they are, it turns out.

The scene then shifts to a nocturnal encounter at the Rajōmon gate (in the ancient city of Heijō-kyō [Nara]) between a lone equestrian samurai and a young woman whom we know to be Shige in her "altered", "reincarnated" form. The man gallantly—albeit with obvious ulterior sexual motives—offers to escort her home through the dark bamboo grove. First seen by we the audience (if not the samurai) as a white-draped, wraith-like entity silently somersaulting over his head contrasted against the jet-blackness of the night sky, he too a short

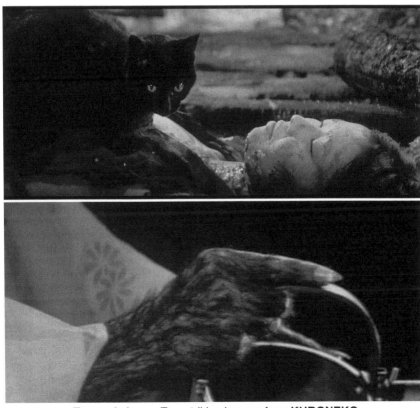

Top and above: Two striking images from **KURONEKO**

Kei Satō as the skeptical Raikō examines the alleged catwoman's arm severed by the sword of Gintoki the samurai

time later comes to the shocked realization—much too late—that she is no ordinary woman. But not before he has accepted an invitation to visit with she and her mother at their not-so-humble abode in the bamboo grove (actually what Wikipedia's entry about the film calls an "illusory mansion", which manifests each night on the site of the women's lowly torched dirt farmers' shack). During his visit, the man repeatedly hears the subdued mewings of an unseen cat, but thinks nothing of it, and his senses become increasingly dulled by drink, which simultaneously stimulates his libido. Well in his cups and feeling amorously inclined, the samurai makes his move on Shige, to which she responds with seemingly passionate compliance. However, after they have finished their loveless lovemaking, Shige proceeds to kill her lover by savagely tearing

out his throat with her teeth (this while distorted bestial sounds akin to those of snarling big cats are heard in the audio mix, albeit not in an overbearingly obvious manner).

The following night, the same basic procedure is then repeated with a second solitary samurai traveler. In this fashion, while her mother-in-law presides from the sidelines, sometimes shown whirling about in a strange solo trance-dance, the vampiristic, succubus-like Shige lures samurai after samurai to their lair, there to first have sex with and then viciously slaughter them as casually as a cat might dispose of mice. Much of the film's first third amounts to little more than a repetitious if beautifully-shot succession of scenes showing the cat-women's murderous *modus operandi*, with

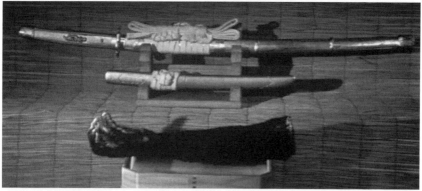

Show of Arms: This grimly comic sight gag is about the only humorous moment to be found in **KURONEKO**!

the end result always being the same: another dead samurai left lying contorted and bloodied amidst the towering bamboo. However, whilst Shige is in the process of luring her fourth potential victim through the grove, suspecting that something is amiss, the samurai attacks her with his sword; whereupon she floats in the air and nimbly scurries up a bamboo trunk like a cat before launching herself at him and killing him with savagely animalistic fury by sinking her teeth/fangs into his neck.

Troubled by the activities of the so-called "spectre" of the Rajōmon (羅城門) gate (whose equivalent was the Rashōmon [羅生門] gate at Heian-kyō [Kyoto]), the fussy Mikado (Hideo Kanze) appoints his governor, the mighty samurai Minamoto no Raikō (Kei Satō [1928-2010]), to dispose of it. A staunch realist who puts no stock in spectres, Raikō asserts with great confidence, "The monster's not a supernatural being. Just an animal or night-prowler!" However, this said, he shortly asks the men in his command, "Is there anyone who will kill the monster?" For wont of any volunteers, Raikō charges a valorous, battle-hardened young samurai named Gintoki (played by *kabuki*-trained actor Kichiemon Nakamura II), freshly returned from the war, with the task: "Get rid of the monster that kills samurai by biting necks".

It develops—coming as no great surprise to us—that Gintoki is no less than Yone's missing son, Shige's husband, who had been pressed into military service and dragged off to join the fray several years prior. While he is passing by the Rajōmon gate late at night, as per her nightly custom the spectral Yone once again appears, requesting he escort her home, as so many other ill-fated young swordsmen have done of late. Upon doing so, he begins to suspect the two strange women are not who they appear to be…in more ways than one. When he demands they reveal their true identities, they vanish, leaving him wondering why these two ghostly beings ("*Monsters!*") have assumed the forms of his loved ones. Having made an unholy pact with dark forces and duty-bound ("Our vow is to kill samurai and suck their blood"), Yone and Shige are sorely conflicted about having to do with Gintoki as they have done to all his predecessors. Now cognizant of both who and what they are, he in turn is reluctant to act on his official orders to slay them. Unable and unwilling to fulfill his pledge to his master, Gintoki returns night after night to the arms of his loving wife, who, like his mother (of whom he asks, "Are you a cat or a ghost?"), can only exist during the hours of darkness between sunset and sunrise. Complications expectedly arise due to this fraternization; not the

She-Cat: Nobuko Otowa in her *kabuki*-style *kaibyō* makeup as Yone…who is *not* a happy kitty

least of which is governor Raikō's increased dissatisfaction with Gintoki for not fulfilling his assigned obligations by acting as the easily-spooked Mikado's "pest controller".

Without divulging too many other major plot points from this point onward, I will mention that when Gintoki takes a swing at one of the creatures and severs one of its forearms with his *katana*, the lopped-off limb promptly transforms from its human form to that of a furry humanoid cat's paw. And the not-exactly-armless (or harmless) if now only one-armed creature wants its missing appendage returned to it; thus provoking the fateful climactic confrontation between mortal and immortal, the alive and the dead. Considering the somberness of all that has preceded this, the melancholically morbid final development—which, for the more hardcore optimist, does have a bittersweet aftertaste—comes as no real revelation, but is no less affecting for it.

As in **ONIBABA**, subtle symbolic suggestion is oftentimes applied with potent force. Even simple natural sounds such as a cricket's chirping and the whisper-like rustling of marsh grasses and tree foliage take on an all-new supernatural life in this melancholy and foreboding context, into which only love dares to intrude with a ray of light and hope…even if both those nobler human emotions ultimately do wind up snuffed-out like candles by the all-consuming darkness and despair pressing in on them from all sides. That said, however, **ONIBABA**, made some four years prior, is debatably even grimmer, more despairing and savagely nihilistic in tone; so by simple contrast, **KURONEKO**'s resolution reads almost like a happy ending in comparison. Director Shindō here reutilized most of his principal behind-the-camera talent from **ONIBABA**. Hikaru Hayashi's mostly minimalist musical compositions effectively underscore the overlying sense of unease, combining sparse percussive elements and such motifs as slightly off-key plucked shamisen strings and/or resonant flutes to emphasize the dark mood. Art direction (by Takashi Marumo), sound (by Tetsuya Ohashi), cinematography (by Kiyomi Kuroda) and editing (by Hisao Enoki) all also modulate in perfect harmony with Shindō's deft direction, which stays spot on the money, keeping extraneous elements to an absolute minimum. Eloquent subtleties (and subtitles, for that matter) abound. Glimpsed in a fleeting C/U insert shot in one scene, mother Yone's ponytail is shown to flick, much like the tail of an angry cat (female hair taking on an unnatural life all its own has long been a recurrent motif in the *kaidan* genre; and more recent years most notably in Hideo Nakata's RING [リング / *Ringu*, 1998] and all its innumerable ripoffs/spinoffs). During another scene a short time later in **KURONEKO**, Shige the daughter's hand is momentarily depicted as a black-furred claw as she serves one of their doomed "guests" some *sake*; the samurai does a double-take at this, evidently unsure—due to being tipsy from the rice wine— if his eyes are playing tricks on him in the dim light. Elsewhere, mother Yone is shown lapping water from a pail then licking her lips in a distinctly cat-like manner, her expression one of broodingly malevolent intent. At another juncture, an inverted reflection of her true, ghostly countenance is fleetingly seen in a mud puddle (similar revelatory shots are to be found in other films of the subgenre). Following the demise of the cat-women's second victim, a raven is shown pecking at the man's torn-throated corpse as it sprawls amidst the bamboo by the cold light of day, the imaginary "cat-house" having once again vanished with the dawn.

The Shindō-penned script makes a number of pointed and bitter criticisms of rigidly-structured feudal era Japan, not the least of which is the ruling class' callous mistreatment of its so-called social inferiors, women especially. Raikō the rakish samurai master is of the opinion that being a samurai is an admirable and enviable thing which can turn even an ordinary man into someone to be both feared and respected by the rulers who require "real men" to fight their wars for them because they are too weak and cowardly to do it for themselves. And of course, courage and prowess in battle makes samurai highly attractive to women (tellingly, as incentive for Gintoki to fulfill his assignment by killing the reputed spectre, Raikō offers him the pick of his personal *geisha* "harem" as a reward). The egotistical, elitist and caste-conscious Raikō, whose attitude towards simple farmers is that they are subhuman and worthy of nothing but contempt, cannot conceive of the idea that anyone—least of all women—should have it in for samurai, those great protectors and providers and mighty heroes of so many songs and legends. However, less honorable samurai (such as those ruffians whose ignoble actions precipitated the cat-demonesses' joint vendetta against all their *bushido* brethren) might get an inflated sense of entitlement due to the power their elevated social standing gave them and thus feel privileged to abuse this power whenever they saw fit. Hence, in this constricting social climate, Yone's and Shige's opposition of their oppressors might well—and indeed, has been—interpreted by some as a kind of feminist backlash against the patriarchal status quo which has used and abused them. Hence, to many viewers, as in so many rape/revenge scenarios, the female protagonists' retributory actions may seem justifiable, even if in this case most of their victims personally had nothing whatsoever to do with the women's sexual violation and murder. Having formed an unholy pact with forces beyond their control, the lingering traces of humanity which still remain in Yone and Shige after their deaths causes them to be at odds with the inhuman sides of themselves, and therein lies the main crux and catalyst of the plot.

Looking a lot younger herein than she had—thanks to being artificially aged via "old hag" makeup—in **ONIBABA**, the charismatic Nobuko Otowa as the matriarch demon-cat well conveys the essence of such a creature without any such too-obvious contrivances as an all-out practical FX monster ever showing up. She scowls, growls and glowers with demonic intensity, but, other than for aforementioned severed non-human limb and a fleeting close-up of the actress with her "cat-face" on—whose theatrical greasepaint makeup strictly adheres to longstanding *kaibyō-eiga* and *kabuki* traditions—that's all we ever see of her feline alter-ego in the flesh. If it was in any other film than this, I might consider that a bit of a cheat, but such discretion and restraint somehow better suits this context; and **KURONEKO** endeavors to be more than "just" a monster movie, anyway, being of equal appeal to fans of arty Japanese cinema in general, and horror movies in particular.

Although it seems most critics tend to regard **ONIBABA** the superior film cinematically speaking, while I do also consider it a great piece of cinema too, for me **KURONEKO** is the odds-on favorite which slightly edges out the former. But both are essential viewing, no matter what kind(s) of cinema you gravitate to most.

HARIMAU JADIAN

("The Weretiger" or *"The Tigerman")*

Malaysia [Singapore?], 1972. D: M. Amin

Here's another unexpected YouTube discovery!

I'm certainly no great expert in the field of Asian cinema, but I do know quite a shitload about Japanese and Hong Kong cinema, have more than a passing familiarity with Filipino films and have seen a number of films of Thai and Indonesian origin…but when it comes to Malaysian movies, I freely admit I'm at a complete loss. So where to start? Although I first ran across it at YT a number of months back and had been intending to give it some coverage here in our 'zine before now, I kept putting it off and putting it off for the simple reason that, with so few points of reference to draw from, I felt like I was virtually flying blind. However, since I've opted to cover a bunch of "cat monster"-themed flicks for the past two issues, I decided it was high time I finally took the plunge into this bit of ultra-obscure exotica from half a world away.

I couldn't find a listing for this film under the current title at the IMDb, although it is up for view in at least two versions on YouTube, but no year of production or release is given at those posts. However, I did find a short clip elsewhere on YT which was dated 1972, so—even though this film was evidently originally shot in B&W and looks a good decade older than that—it's the year I've decided to go with (*filemklasikmalaysia.blogspot.ca* confirms it, so that's good enough for me). Having used online software to automatically translate the original title, I got the somewhat surreal-sounding "Invented Tiger" (YT's translator gives it as "Imitation Tiger"); although an online Malay-to-English dictionary I referred to (@ *imtranslator.net*) gave it as "The Creation of the Tiger", which sounds a bit too formal/literal for my liking. Judging by what I saw elsewhere via doing a Google search, *harimau jadian* evidently can also translate to "The Tigerman", or even "The Weretiger"…so take your pick; but it's either of those two lattermost translations I most favor, for obvious reasons (this here 'zine is called *Monster!*, after all).

When I first ran across **HARIMAU JADIAN** at YT and didn't know better, I thought it might be P. Ramlee's **SITORA HARIMAU JADIAN** (1964; which I covered in my "Hamburger Movies" piece back in *M!* #6 [see also pages p.57-63 this ish]); however, after doing some extra research, it appears as though that much-sought-after '64 film has since become irretrievably lost, more's the pity.

The topmost three screen captures show the film's main title card, plus directly below it are two shots of the cuddly were-tiger that is briefly seen before the opening credits roll. Directly above, the creature can be seen emerging from its jungle prison after being set free by the human hero

Top: A "lacerated" (!) victim of Abang the were-leopard. **Above:** The caged creature in its "fully-transformed" state, looking a bit glum

As for our present film under review, its *pengarah* ("director") M. Amin (*née* Muhammad Amin bin Ihsan, 1924-2003) was also an actor who had co-starred in B. Narayan Rao's now-believed-lost Malay horror film **PONTIANAK** (*"The Vampire"*, 1957, Singapore), which was a sequel to the same director's **DENDAM PONTIANAK** (*"Revenge of the Vampire"*), another Singaporean-made Malay-language film from '57. As with those two titles, **HARIMAU JADIAN** was produced by the highly prolific Cathay Keris Film—it was reportedly their 126th production—a company for which the present film's director Amin directed numerous other titles.

Although in what precise historical period the narrative is set is indeterminate (no evidence of any modern technology is seen, so my guess is the setting is at least a couple centuries or more in the past), the established milieu is a typical rural community in the Peninsular Malaysian state of Johor, consisting of thatched-roofed houses on stilts set amidst dense tropical rain forest, which is alive with the twittering of birds, the chirping of insects and sounds of other jungle wildlife. Thanks to a very "loose" (i.e., only semi-intelligible) automated translation of a Malay synopsis I found online, I think I managed to deduce

the main thrust of the plot, give or take the odd "subtle" detail; not that there appeared to be too much in the way of subtlety on display here, from what I could tell while watching it in untranslated form.

For cuckolding the village elder—whose wife, fearing her hubby's wrath, saves herself by crying rape when she and her lover are about to be caught in the act of adultery—the cuckold hightails it into the surrounding jungle. Torch-bearing villagers attempt to hunt down the tomcattin' fugitive like an animal; however, the sly cuckold himself, who, such is his arrogance, is even assisting with the manhunt, accuses the wrong man for the dirty deed, whereupon this innocent victim of circumstance (evidently named "Abang" and presumably played by the top-billed Rohani Yusoff?) is given a retributory group pounding on the spot. Having been beaten bloody, the wrongfully accused man is then brought before the elder's wife whom he has supposedly raped. She bears false witness yet again by claiming that he is indeed her rapist. Further injury is then added to insult when Abang is strung up by his wrists and subjected to a punitive public caning via bamboo pole, this administered one after the other by a number of local men, all swinging full-force at his back (I counted around 50 blows! If not for the unconvincing staging and the broad histrionics and overdone body language of the participants, this scene of extreme corporal punishment might have appeared genuinely disturbing).

Not surprisingly rendered unconscious by his brutal treatment at the hands of his accusers/abusers, afterwards Abang is thrown into a local river, presumably to drown. When, clinging tenaciously to some driftwood, Abang is spotted drifting downstream by some young washerwomen (including our sexy heroine, actress' name unknown) from another village, he is rescued and nursed back to health. Having since become romantically entwined, when our hero and heroine subsequently "consummate" their mutual attraction, their love scene is abruptly cut short as though something got unceremoniously censored; but judging by what remains, I highly doubt anything even remotely resembling nudity—let alone actual sexual activity—was on display in the uncut print (if indeed it was cut; sure looks like). All we are left with are a shot of the lovers' "passionately" interlocked fingers, followed by C/U's of their "ecstatic" faces, rocking suggestively to and fro…and that's all she wrote! The only nipples seen are those on our husky hero's moobs.

Later, after Abang paddles off downriver in his dugout canoe on an indeterminate quest, while making a pit-stop on land en route, he comes across a tiger caught in a bamboo cage in the jungle. Although fleeting stock shots of an actual tiger are crudely cut in here, the one in the cage is clearly only an oversized stuffed puppet, and when this captive "creature" begins to speak to our human hero in Malay with an eerie echo effect, this is where—approaching the halfway point of the runtime—things start to get more interesting. Abang cautiously sets the caged animal free, whereupon it abruptly assumes its human form, transforming from a crawling "tiger-skin rug" into an upright man (c/o a crude editing effect, evidently accomplished in-camera). Interestingly enough, a certain aspect of this part of the story (i.e., the fearsome beast's gratitude at being liberated by the weaker creature) is rather reminiscent of the Aesop's fable "The Lion and the Mouse", and like all Mr. Aesop's fables, this film also comes with a built-in moral at its conclusion.

In exchange for setting him free, following a "rigorous" training program which amongst other things involves him being buried up to his neck in the earth and getting rained on by a raging thunderstorm, the grateful tigerman endows its rescuer with the ability to transform himself into a big cat, too (albeit one with leopard spots, rather than tiger stripes like his teacher; when in their human forms, both men sport loud print "pajamas" whose patterns vaguely evoke the markings found on the pelts of their respective feline namesakes). The source of Abang's newfound power is a tiger fang pendant (at sight of which, an old man later asks of him, "*Harimau jadian?*" as per the title). Although he has been strictly instructed by his tigerman teacher never to use his transforming ability for evil purposes, Abang opts to avenge himself on those responsible for engineering the frame-up which saw him brutalized and permanently banished from his home village. Afflicted with literal "cat scratch fever" (if you will), he goes on a kill-crazy rampage which seldom appears even the remotest bit convincing, but at least it's depicted with energetic enthusiasm. After Abang is captured and caged while in his leopard form, his alleged rape victim, the elder's wayward wife, at last confesses her wrongdoing; whereafter she is publicly spurned by her husband for her faithlessness and he then proceeds to let Abang the captured leopardman loose to take his revenge on her. As she makes her terrified run through the jungle to escape his wrath, Abang—still in his bestial form—pursues and kills her. Courtesy of some very rough editing/bad continuity here, we don't see her actual killing, just a fleeting glimpse of her bloodied body with her now-human-form killer standing over it in the aftermath (once again, as with that earlier "sex" scene, some footage seems

to have been chopped out, this time possibly due to violent content [?]).

Following this cathartic satiation of his bloodlust, Abang is confronted by the tigerman his teacher, who is angry at him for misusing his powers. Assuming their feline forms, the man-tiger and man-leopard then do battle in a furious flurry of spots and stripes, their combat framed in such a way that most of it is hidden by underbrush so as to hopefully disguise the fact that what we're witnessing is merely two guys done up in fluffy cat-suits rolling around (the simple blurriness of the upload I watched only added to the general indistinctness of the action, not just here but elsewhere too). In mid-bout, they both pop back to their human selves. Then, much like the final fight between the hero and the head villain seen in many an HK MA flick before and since, the teacher and his student continue to pound the tar out of each other, if shown mostly in long shot and with very little finesse evident in their fighting technique. Produced at the height of the Asian (indeed, virtually international) martial arts movie craze, **HARIMAU JADIAN** has a token earlier scene of MA training right out of a Hong Kong 'fu actioner (although the fighting style seen here is a lot sloppier and less graceful, combining Muay Thai-type moves and streetfight-style brawling). When in human form our leopardman Abang engages enemies hand-to-hand, his slashing blows leaving claw-like scratch marks on their skin. He goes into a savage frenzy while defending himself against a group of attackers in the jungle. The climactic deciding duel between Abang and his man-tiger master leads into the downbeat conclusion and the film closes with that moral message I mentioned above.

Exaggerated and amplified, the werecats' ferocious booming roars sound rather like those for monsters in a Japanese *kaiju eiga*; the same foreshortened sound effect repeated over and over again, like it's on a tape loop. The cutely cuddlesome critters rather reminded me of some oddball hybrid of an XL ambulatory plush toy and an Asian "lion dance" costume. In fact, back when he was but a nipper my now-teenage nephew used to own a plush big cat toy (a leopard rather than a tiger) which had a similar cuddly-cutesy look to it as the walking Tigger toys seen here. Despite their lack of anatomical correctness in anything other than the rudiments, they are kept on such unabashed display that you can't help feeling a certain affection towards them. The musical score by Wan Lim Chye (evidently of Chinese descent?) mostly sounds like typically melodramatic orchestration, albeit with a more exotic Asiatic tinge at times, incorporating tribal percussion and sometimes eerie swooshing/fluttering sounds which add

Chik, M. Shahdan, Zaharah Omar, Habsah, Buang, Noor Kuda and Man Goyang. Although I can find no listing for a Rohani Yusoff at the IMDb, an actor named Rohani Yusof (less one f) has a credit there for but a single film, made the same year as our present title: namely Danu Umbara's apparent crime actioner **PENGEJARAN KE NERAK** (*"Chase to Hell"*, 1972, Indonesia). On an indirectly related note, **TIGER MAN** (1978, USA) was a MA actioner directed by Matt Cimber and starring Don Wong, but isn't about a literal tigerman. Buddhadev Dasgupta's **BAGH BAHADUR** (a.k.a. **THE TIGER MAN**, 1989, India) is a non-monster Bengali/Hindi drama.

EVIL CAT
(凶猫 / *Xiong mao*)

Hong Kong, 1987. D: Dennis Yu

Master Cheung says in subtitle: *"He is an evil-spirited cat!"* (But then, aren't we all…?)

This comedic horror fantasy was co-produced and directed by Dennis Yu (he who helmed the nasty rape/revenge psycho-killer thriller **THE BEASTS** [山狗 / *Shan kou*, a.k.a. **FLESH AND THE BLOODY TERROR**, 1980, HK] and the creepy occult horror film **THE IMP** [凶榜 / *Xiong bang*, 1981, HK]), and was written by Jing Wong (screenwriter of Ngai Choi Lam's crazy horror **THE SEVENTH CURSE** [原振俠與衛斯理 / *Yuan zhen-xia yu Wei Si-li*, 1986, HK], starring Chow Yun Fat, and writer-director of **KUNG FU CULT MASTER** [倚天屠龍記之魔教教主 / *Yi tin to lung gei: Moh gaau gaau jue*, a.k.a. **THE EVIL CULT**, 1993, HK], starring Jet Li and co-directed by Sammo Hung). Like much of Yu's and Wong's material from the time, **EVIL CAT** is so typical of the era in which it was made, and it's a shame they just don't make 'em like this anymore; although, that said, the present film might have turned out *so-o-o* much better than it did…

At an excavation, workers unearth a huge slab of stone covered in hieroglyphics, and when they remove this stopper they find a deep shaft sunken into the ground beneath it. During a flashback sequence we learn that an "evil cat" demon had been consigned to this wholly unholy hole four centuries before by a fearless Daoist priest, who then trapped it beneath the prayer-covered stone to keep it there. Subsequently, the action now shifting back to contemporary times, an as-yet-unseen (quote) "strange creature"—possibly one with cat-like characteris-

to the oddball ambience. Lowbrow comedy relief is of the slapstick and scatological varieties (i.e., a man gibbering in comical terror at sight of one of the "monsters", and another with the shits urgently running into the bush to relieve himself, then sniffing his fingers afterwards).

At the time I first spotted it there, the rip of **HARIMAU JADIAN** uploaded at YT had scored less than 200 views and only 1 "Like" (!). When I checked in again some months later while preparing this review, as of September 6, 2014, the total number of views had since increased to a whopping (and kinda *eerie*) 666; but still with only a single "thumbsup", though. While there is very little in the way of special effects and practical makeup is virtually nonexistent—yep, pretty much all we get are those awkwardly mobile plush toys!—there is a pleasingly and unselfconsciously naïve quality to the entire production which I found rather charming and difficult to resist. Given the option, I would have much preferred to watch Ramlee's aforementioned **SITORA HARIMAU JADIAN** instead; but Amin's similarly-titled **HARIMAU JADIAN** proved to be a pleasant enough consolation prize nonetheless. By all means go check it out on YT; this motley, moth-eaten moggy needs all the likes it can get. Who knows, maybe you might even *love* it…

NOTES: Since I could find no listing for this at the IMDb, I figured I'd list some of the other principal cast members: also including S. Azam, Osman Zailani, Omar Hitam, Dollah Sarawak, Din Wan

tics, perchance?—rips up a couple of victims at a maximum security high-rise office building before, having taken possession of the building's CEO Mr. Fan (Stuart Ong), it disappears into the night. Ballsy TV news reporter Siu-chuen Cheung ("Joanne Tang", a.k.a. Tang Lai Ying) promptly gets on the case, as does Inspector Wu (chubby Eric Tsang-type Wong Ching, providing still more unneeded "comic relief" as the bumbling, cowardly detective; for instance, he barfs—not just once, not even twice, but fully *thrice*—after witnessing the bloodied remains of one of the cat creature's victims). As to Siu-chuen's reasonable-enough suspicions that some sort of big cat escaped from a zoo or circus might be the perpetrator, Insp. Wu says dismissively and erroneously, "I think it must be just a big dog. Nothing special". That latter description might well be applied to the film itself, which, while far from an all-out woofer, is a tad too high in mediocrity to warrant a glowing appraisal; but that isn't to say it doesn't have a goodly supply of memorable moments, even if in sum total it doesn't quite equal some of its individual parts.

Out to put a stop to the evil cat, expert *Mao Shan* man, the evil-fighting mystic Master Cheung (seasoned actor-director Chia-liang Liu, a.k.a. Lau Kar Leung [1936-2013])—who is none other than Siu-chuen's father and is battling cancer, it develops—gives the young, Rolls Royce-driving rookie rent-a-cop (i.e., security guard) hero Long (Mark Cheng) a magic charm to ward off evil...*evil cats*, especially. We learn that the possessed cat has nine lives ("This is the last life of the evil-spirited cat"), and returns from the beyond once each generation in order to fulfill another stage of its life cycle (interestingly enough, in its rudiments this plot detail is more than a little reminiscent of **THE CATMAN OF PARIS** [1946, USA], right down to the 50-year

timespan between the creature's reappearances). A shot showing blood oozing under a door may have been a direct nod to Lewton/Tourneur's eloquent feline-themed thriller **THE LEOPARD MAN** (1943, USA), or it may just have been a simple coinkydink...I tend to think the latter might be the case, but you never know.

Dressed in a business suit and augmented with dubbed-on leopard-like snarls, the cat demon-possessed Fan character leaps around with fantastically feline agility, and at one point is caught nocturnally poaching a koi carp, which it/he has snatched from a fishpond with its/his teeth (eating raw fish apparently gives the cat demon within him its power, you see). When he attacks our hero Long, Fan does so using some fittingly "tiger claw"-style kung fu moves. However, when he/it makes the mistake of grabbing him by his sacred talisman, the catman gets blasted backwards by the force of goodness contained within it. Having survived first being run over and then blasted by an exploding car, Fan subsequently returns unscathed to re-menace Long, whom he momentarily levitates using telekinetic energy when his eyes glow red. Leave it to Long's quick-thinking mom to save his ass by hurling a handy Buddha statue at Fan, who consequently hurtles through an apartment complex window and, unlike a cat, doesn't land on his feet. However, once again Mr. Fan bounces back, resuming his official position as head honcho of the haunted holdings company.

Master Cheung informs Long, who has volunteered to be his adherent and Mao Shan student, how to dispose of the creature: using a sacred bow which fires "magical ancestral arrows", of which a mere three still remain in the entire world ("They're made of God of Thunder's charms", he explains, inevi-

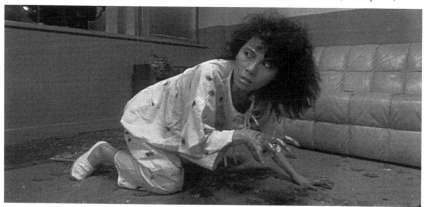

Tina the feline demon-possessed office worker runs wild! (I do believe the actress playing her might be Shu-yuan Hsu, but I'm not 100% certain.)

Terrible Tina goes all "**LIFEFORCE**" on their asses when she attacks a hospital emergency unit and sucks them dry of their living energy

tably prompting memories in viewers of a certain '70s hard rock hit by Kiss). A direct heart-shot is needed to put a stop to the monster. Another weapon in Cheung's magical arsenal is the "peach rapier", a sacred sword presumably not intended for slicing fruit with…although, that said, nothing much else is ever done with it, either. Regardless of all his fancy weaponry, proving that he's no slouch at unarmed combat should need arise when a bunch of bullying rent-a-cops lay some police-style brutality on his aging ass using their billy-clubs, Master—wearing a "wife-beater"-style vest (i.e., muscle shirt)—retaliates with some magic MA moves that put the power-tripping bastards in their places toot sweet.

As for Master's apprentice, tall, dark and handsome romantic leading man Mark Cheng was later cast in a far less wholesome light as the fetishistic serial rapist of "Ivan Lai" / Kai-ming Lai's Category III erotic thriller **THE PEEPING TOM** (赤足惊魂 /

Chik juk ging wan, a.k.a. **BARE FOOT THRILL-ER**, 1996, HK). So typical of the era, in our present film a lowbrow phallic joke is made about the hero's name, which, while it itself is only short, implies he must be (ahem) *lengthy* where it counts. During one lively sequence, Long our hunky and presumably well-hung hero shatters an aquarium all over the floor then electrifies the spilled water by throwing a table lamp at it, causing Fan the catman (still entirely in human form) to get zapped, and while he is being electrocuted, Master shows up to zip a magic arrow into his/its heart, whereupon the creature's face glows red and it explodes, releasing the malevolent spirit from within. However, this evil essence still lives, and shortly moves on to inhabit the body of Fan's personal assistant Tina instead, the cat's spirit matter streaming into her through the roof of her home as a blue beam (which appears to enter via her nightgown-draped crotch!). Some **THE EN-TITY** (1982, USA)-styled poltergeist activity also

Despite the dazzling optical FX light show, dark forces are afoot as the evil cat creature possesses its latest unwilling human host

figures in this scene. Having become well and truly infused by the evil cat's energy, the woman becomes its latest carrier.

From right out of nowhere, we are then subjected to a hideous, badly lip-synched—if mercifully brief—'80s-style pop song being performed at a recording studio by some fictitious teenybop-pop idol named Vincent, who shortly becomes the human-form cat-woman's first victim. Out for some (*sorry!*) pussy, upon being picked up by her in her flash Mercedes for a quickie in the backseat, he gets more than he bargained for after removing her panties when she proceeds to bite off his oral organ while they are necking ("I'll give back your tounge [*sic*]", she says in subtitle after removing from between her teeth his freshly-severed slurper, which shan't be used to make this pussy purr). In a tense game of cat-and-mouse, she thereafter stalks the terrified tongueless singer—there may well be a message in there some-where!—through the local monsoon drains, toying with him like a kitten with a ball of yarn while leaping and bounding all over the joint c/o some more patently obvious wire-work than usual for the time (while invisible piano wires were responsible for some stunning stunt-work at the time, here the actors attached to them sometimes merely appear to be bouncing around like yo-yos). After she receives a phone call about Vincent's demise, Siu-chuen our heroine announces, "He was killed by an ani-mal-like creature" (as opposed to *what*, exactly?! A *non*-animal-like creature, perhaps? It doesn't take a zoologist to know there ain't no such animal!).

Now down to their last two arrows, Master and Long track the killer catwoman back to her digs. Succu-bus-like, in her alluring human form—"nude", even if no real nudity is shown throughout—Tina entices Long by beckoning to him from the bushes. After wasting one of their remaining projectiles when it doesn't fly true and misses its target's heart, striking her closer to the shoulder instead, Tina the catwom-an is saved by advent of the HK Police, who wound Master in the hand with a pistol-shot and then ap-prehend both he and Long, having wrongly assumed they were attempting to murder the "innocent" woman, who makes with the appropriate hysterics to sell the illusion to the fuzz. His guiding *si-foo* now temporarily out of commission and with but a single arrow left, the responsibility predictably falls on his inexperienced apprentice Long to put paid to the killer kitty once and for all…or *does* it? Despite setting things up to go this way, the plot takes anoth-er apparently random turn when Master does indeed meet his date with the evil cat, resulting in a magical martial arts duel between the man and the still-not-yet-transformed catwoman, who nonetheless has

the ability to deploy her detachable forearms like missiles to assault her opponent (!). The big irony is that the evil cat's spirit, while still inside Tina, forces its way into Master and attempts to assume control of him, too. After he blows to bits—evident-ly from the internal pressure build-up—while trying to resist the cat's domination, things get figuratively messier still when the demon's essence proves to have jumped ship yet again…

Most unfortunately, the title creature isn't seen in its more monstrous form until late into the narrative; by that I mean *real* late into it…like, try within the last six minutes or so (if it arrived any later, it might just as well not have bothered showing up at all! But then cats are known to come and go as they please, after all, so perhaps it fits the character). When it does finally make its appearance, it looks about as ferocious as your average cast-member of *Cats* with its frizzy, teased-up '80s "big hair", fuzzy face and whiskers. One of the only four user reviews for the film at IMDb says the transformed kitty-monster looks like a "really cheap Thundercat", from the 1985-89 kids' TV cartoon show *Thundercats* (which I've never seen, but since another user review also compares the she-cat seen here to a certain Cheetara character from that show, I can only assume there must be some truth to the comparison). I can't un-derstand why they chose to make the creature white instead of a more logical black one, but perhaps they did it for the sake of "irony", I don't know. And even after showing up so late to the party, it still doesn't stick around long, and both the evil cat and **EVIL CAT** are all over and done with in a far too cursory fashion for my liking…but such is life (in this case the ninth one of a cat).

The liveliness of **EVIL CAT**'s action sequences provides at least some compensation for its lame-ness in the monster department. For instance, whilst in possession of its female host, after she/it gets loose from the ER while undergoing surgery to remove that aforementioned arrow in her chest, thus restored to close to full-strength Tina (**LIFE-**

Tang Lai Ying does her cutesy "Cheetara" impression as the fully-morphed feline demoness

FORCE-style) proceeds to increase it still further by sucking the life out of not only the surgical team, but also that of a cop, too, thrusting her forearm clear through a second one shortly thereafter. She then goes on a crazed killing spree at the local cop-shop, ramming one cop's face through the—obviously only plastic—bottle of a water cooler then pile-driving another's head clear off his shoulders (!) like nothing. A direct shot in her forehead from a .357 Magnum at close range fails to faze Tina even slightly, let alone actually stop her dead in her tracks, while a subsequent thorough perforating by a broadside of police M-16's and .38's likewise barely even musses her hair, even if it does rather mess up her outfit. This was/is the kind of looniness which HK action cinema fans couldn't/can't get enough of! Because it was made at the height of the HK action movie craze as well as at the height of the HK horror movie craze, some purely gratuitous car

Catfish: Stuart Ong as Mr. Fan has a midnight sushi snack in **EVIL CAT**

stunts and pyrotechnics are tossed in for good measure in hopes of cornering both markets. During the period in which this was produced, pretty much as soon as you laid eyes on a glass-topped coffee table in a Hong Kong action/exploitation flick, you could bank on it getting smashed to bits in the very near future. In **EVIL CAT**, although at an earlier point a stuntman does indeed get body-slammed through the top of one, causing a flashy splash of glass shards, when we see a second such piece of furniture placed in plain sight later on, it surprisingly enough survives intact! (Possibly smashing that first one put them over-budget…?)

DP Arthur Wong's agile cinematography OD's on shadow and blue lighting. Special optical FX by John Ting and Jackie Tang include a giant ethereal cat-face superimposed over a night sky; which quite frankly looks like something out of a Pat Benatar video, that's how chintzy it is. Gruesome gore is juxtaposed with goofy gags (for instance, at one point a severed hand is used to make a cheap sight-gag). As with so many frenetic, anything-goes '80s HK flicks, the script—which has plenty of room to swing a cat in it, and then some—often seems to be making itself up as it goes along, chopping and changing from one development and idea to the next with seemingly random spontaneity and little regard for logic or cohesion. One of the film's strongest points, Wing-fai Law's drony/whiny electronic score at times creates an eerily unsettling mood which ideally complements all the scenes of people creeping about in dark places looking for who-knows-what. Although the print of **EVIL CAT** I watched for the purposes of this review came equipped with English soft-subs, riddled as they were with so many typographical errors and bad grammar (e.g., "What a bitter satire?", "He fonds of a fantasy life", "But its sinister is difficult to defeat", "I can predict that I'll tonight", and "You such a disgusting evil", etc.), they well-recreated the feel of those oft-hilarious and sometimes just plain bizarre/surreal hard subtitles seen on innumerable HK theatrical/video prints back in the '80s and '90s. The subs on Fortune Star's DVD zip by so quickly that you need to be a speed-reader in order to keep up with them, so a momentary pause and/or rewind may well be in order periodically.

In regards to the film as a whole? Don't go in expecting too much, and you ought to be sufficiently entertained to overlook its numerous shortcomings. My main gripe would be that they could have done so much better with the title creature than they did(n't); such as making it about ten times more ferocious in both its appearance and behavior, for instance. As semi-tame as it is, though, **EVIL CAT** should perhaps have just been called "**BAD KITTY**" instead.

THE [LOST] TIGERMAN OF KUALA LUMPUR

by Steve Fenton

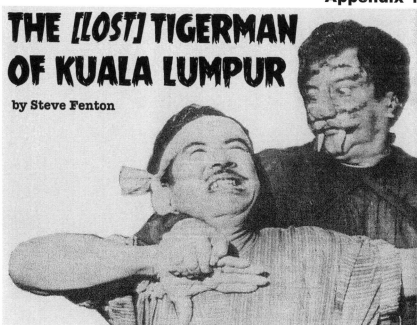

Right off the top of my "Hamburger Movies" list back in *Monster!* #6, I expended a quite longish paragraph about the long-AWOL 1964 Malaysian monster movie **SITORA HARIMAU JADIAN** (variously translated as "Sitora, Tigerman", "Sitora the Man-Tiger" and even "Sitora the Weretiger"), but because some additional information became available since then—some hazily lo-rez but most welcome pictures included, which is a real plus—I figured I'd do a bit of an update as a tie-in with all my other Asiatic "cat monster"-themed stuff this ish.

Almarhum (or Allahyarham) Tan Sri P. Ramlee (*née* Teuku Zakaria bin Teuku Nyak Puteh), typically known just as plain old P. Ramlee for short, was born in Penang, Malaysia on March 22, 1929 and eventually rose to become one of the greatest and most beloved showbiz superstars that Asia has ever produced; whose popularity seems greater now than it ever was. As an artist/entertainer, the multi-talented, seemingly do-it-all Ramlee wore many hats over the course of his meteoric career, including those of singer/songwriter, actor, novelist and filmmaker (etc.); most of whose canon in that lattermost capacity I freely admit I have little or no interest in seeing, but I don't consider **SITORA** a "hamburger" of the most appetizing order without good reason: it's an all-out monster movie from a film industry whose excursions into such territory are comparatively rare, which makes it all the more unfortunate that

PENGEMBARAAN MENGKAGUMKAN FIKIRAN!
Pengalaman sa-orang doktor di-desa yang di-kuasai oleh harimau jadian! Padat dengan peristiwa2 yang jarang terdapat di-lain2 persembahan!

P. RAMLEE

SITORA
HARIMAU JADIAN

(THE TIGERMAN)

Dengan Mahmud June * Rosmawati * Ali Rahman memperkenalkan Fazilyaton * Yusof Surya * Idris Hashim

it's become seemingly permanently unavailable for viewing. (But now that I've said that, just you wait and see: a deluxe special edition Blu-ray complete with a pristine, fully-restored print, missing scenes and loaded with making-of featurettes will probably be released next month, just to prove me wrong... But I say, *bring it on!* Although it'd be great if it

Scratching Post: P. Ramlee as Dr. Effendi, in his transformed state

turned up in *any* form or condition, even a cruddy fifth-generation VHS dub.)

In *M!* #6, I incorrectly stated that **SITORA** was the only horror/monster film for which Ramlee handled direction. However, I have since learned—all it took was a quick pop-in at the IMDb to find out—that Malay Film Productions' **CURSE OF THE OILY MAN** (*Sumpah orang minyak*, 1958, Singapore/Malaysia) not only starred Ramlee as Bongkok the title character—a hunchback who becomes magically transformed into something *worse*—but was also scripted and directed by him; although, considering the less permissive time in which it was made, it goes without saying that it takes a much more subdued approach to its material than did Ho Meng-hua's later, lewder and more lurid take on a similar scenario, the Shaw Brothers' **THE OILY MANIAC** (油鬼子 / *You gui zi*, 1976, Hong Kong), starring Danny Lee in the title part. While **CURSE OF THE OILY MAN**'s entry at the IMDb describes that film as a "Drama | Fantasy | Thriller", it also definitely has some pronounced horror/ monster elements (if you don't believe me, check it out for yourself: there are at least two different uploads of it on view at YouTube; simply do a search for it under its original Malay title given above). It won an award for Best Photography at the *5 Festival Filem Asia* / 5th Asian Film Festival in Manila in '58. Hyped on ads as "The Incredible Story of Malaya's Most Fantastic Character!" the monochromatic film brims with moody, brooding atmosphere (expect coverage of it here in *Monster!* sometime soon... possibly even next ish). Ads for original theatrical prints also made mention of "Superimposed English Subtitles" (once a common procedure for Malaysian

films, as with those from Hong Kong too); but unfortunately none are to be found on either of those aforementioned versions at YT.

Having directed some sixteen films under the auspices of the mighty Shaw Brothers conglomerate at their Malay Film Productions wing whilst living and working in Singapore, upon his return to Malaysia in 1964, from March of that year until '72, Ramlee, then aged 35, began working for Merdeka ("Independent") Film Productions—formed in 1961 by H.M. Shah and his business partner, Ho Ah Loke—a company in which Ramlee was a major shareholder and under whose banner he helmed a total of eighteen films, starting with the now-missing monster movie **SITORA HARIMAU JADIAN** (which shouldn't be confused with a completely unrelated 1972 Malay film called **HARIMAU JADIAN** [see p. 49], made by the rival Cathay Keris outfit [one can only assume its makers were well aware of the then-presumably still extant Ramlee film of similar title?]). Interestingly enough, Merdeka's premises (at Ulu Klang / Hulu Kelang, in the Gombak region of Selangor) were situated close by to a zoo whose animal occupants included...*tigers!* As with other Asian nations too, the tiger is Malaysia's national animal. A stylized pair of them—interestingly enough, standing on their hind legs, like men (possibly even weretigers?!)—flank the Malaysian national coat of arms, the *Jata Megara*, which was officially adopted in 1963—so these creatures have clearly exerted a powerful influence on the continent's culture.

Evidently finding himself in some sort of a creative slump at the time, Ramlee was trying to come up

58

with viable ideas for his next film. According to reports, he was inspired by such Hollywood horrors as **WEREWOLF OF LONDON** (1935) and **THE WOLF MAN** (1941) to come up with a variation of a were-creature tale slanted toward a more Asian sensibility and market. We like to think it was the roars he heard coming from the tiger cage of the zoo next door that prompted him to write a script about a tigerman: the sort of fantastical creature which in Malaysian/Indonesian folklore typically subsists via drinking human blood (I can find no reference to the one in the film doing this, however. But, due to censorial constraints in its country of origin at that time, maybe this unsavory aspect was tactfully downplayed in the scenario, possibly only implied [?]. However, the monsters seen in our attendant grainy photographs most certainly do have vampire-like fangs, so you never know).

In 1966, the Shaw Bros. assumed a controlling interest in Merdeka (aforementioned Malay Film Productions went bust in '67, some three years after Ramlee "jumped ship" over to Merdeka). Ramlee's final film under the Merdeka banner was the at times bawdy, everything-but-the-kitchen-sink comedy adventure **LAKSAMANA DO RE MI** (1972). He died due to cardiac arrest on May 29, 1973, at the age of only 44; following which loss of their greatest asset Merdeka's business interests accordingly suffered a drastic setback, him being their biggest breadwinner. After making the period sword-swinging martial arts revenge actioner **LOCENG MAUT** (*"Death Knell"*) in 1976—a Shaw Bros. co-production featuring Malaysian action star Hussein Abu Hassan, co-directed by Kuei Chi Hung; fight instructors on the film included the many-laureled Ching Siu Tung and Lau Kar Leung a.k.a. Chia-liang Liu (star of this ish's furiously furry HK horror **EVIL CAT** [凶猫 / *Xiong mao*, 1987])—the studios shut up shop in 1980, this after they produced their final effort, Othman Hafsham's comedy **ADIK MANJA** (*"Dear Child"* [1979]). In 1985 the studios were bought up by the local National Film Development Corporation (FINAS), who preserved the buildings for their historical/posterity value and converted them to offices while still retaining the Merdeka name.

Following its initial screenings in the year of its production—original theatrical release was in November '64 (then aged 5, I was living in Singapore as an RAF "base brat" at that time, running with local Malay/Chinese street kids, as it happens)—SITORA apparently secured at least one domestic Malaysian TV airing sometime during the '70s, but hasn't been seen since, even if it has most definitely been heard of, and many Ramlee fans and Malaysian film buffs now seem to regard it as some sort of cinematic Holy Grail ripe for rediscovery...although all evidence seems to point to it being irretrievably lost

atu babak pergadohan antara dua ekor harimau jadian (P. Ramlee dan lahmood June) dalam filem Si-To a yang akan di-tayangkan di-pang-gong? Shaw tengah malam ini.

Dr. Effendi, played by P. Ramlee, plies his profession in **SITORA**

(but "Never say never", as they say; I refer you back to what I said in the second paragraph off-the-top about it potentially showing up on Blu when you least expect it …but don't hold your breath, tiger).

A tie-in novelization was published by the Penerbitan Angkatan Baru (*"New Force Publications"*) imprint of Kuala Lumpur in 1965, and, because it was illustrated with numerous stills from the film, is now one of the few remaining sources of images from it, including most of those seen hereabouts. Because the original novel was written in Bahasa Kebangsaan (then the national language of some Malaysian states), its writing style has since become considered dated; hence, for its 2012 Malay reprint by Amir Muhammad's native Buku Fixi (*"Fixi Books"*) publishing house, certain spellings and grammar were updated to better suit more modern usage, presumably in the interests of generating higher sales by attracting a younger consumer demographic (Ramlee evidently has a broad fan-base of more youthful followers). According to one Khairul H. in a May 2012 online English-language review of the book: "If the film itself is gone for good then reading about it would be the next best thing. And indeed it was. Without the reportedly cheap visual effects to prejudice one's feelings about it, the prose version of **SITORA** proved to be a not-so-bad stab by P. Ramlee at the horror genre. The lack of audiovisuals would also help the reader appreciate the social commentary […] it is refreshing to be reading flowery-theatrical-who-speaks-like-that-in-real-life Malay once again… I confess my 4-star rating for this book was influenced more by my appreciation of anything P. Ramlee and the serendipity of finally having able [sic] to read, if not watch, *Sitora Harimau Jadian* than by the quality of the story itself. Maybe a 3 for the story, plus 1 star for the historical value of a lost, allegedly bad, classic".

Ramlee's grandson is reportedly the recipient of royalties from sales of the reprinted edition. I "borrowed"—ta kindly, peeps!—most of the images seen here from Buku Fixi's Facebook page for their reprint of the book (at *SITORA HARIMAU JADIAN - Sebuah Novel P. Ramlee*), which according to reports wasn't the source of the film's Ramlee-penned screenplay, but was written by him after the fact, or possibly simultaneously, as a merchandising tie-in with the film. As of October 2013, a stage play adapted from the novel was planned for the theatre at the University of Malaya. I'm not sure if it was actually performed or how many (if any) performances there were, but I can only hope they didn't do with the material what the makers of *Evil Dead: The Musical* did! (That is to say, turn it into "high camp" for hipsters, complete with cheesy song numbers, possibly along the lines of Andrew Lloyd Webber.) However, I digress: back to the original film…

Ramlee's starring role as Dr. Effendi—that's how his name is spelled in the book, but I've also seen it elsewhere either misspelled or perhaps alternately transliterated as "Affendi" or "Afendi" (see quoted excerpt below)—was reportedly a quite typically Hollywoodian "medico" character, evidently with at least some either latent or overt madness in him, as befitting typical Western "mad doctor" tropes. The word "Effendi" (or variations thereof in Arabic, Turkish, Persian and Greek, etc.) is of course an honorary title bestowed upon men warranting respect, and that choice of surname seems to have been a simplistic bit of symbolism on screenwriter/novelist Ramlee's part; much as with the name of the film's titular character Sitora (derived from *"tora"*, the Japanese word for tiger; the author was reputedly fluent in said language). This seems about the right place to delve deeper into **SITORA**'s story, so here we go (fingers crossed)…

Do bear in mind that I pieced together/reworded the bulk of the synopsis given in the next two paragraphs from a sometimes rather awkwardly-worded English-language story outline which I found *somewhere* online; however, I've since misplaced the link to the source, otherwise I'd cite it here (I honestly now have no clue where I originally found it!), and just too many links—many score, if not hundreds—popped up when I Googled the movie's title, so I didn't feel like wading back through trying to re-find the one for the synopsis I mainly used for reference here (all I originally did was click on a whole pile at random, looking for what I could find at the most promising sites and copying/pasting raw data). But it was about the most complete plot breakdown I could come up with that wasn't all in Malay, which would turn to largely indecipherable gibberish (mostly for simple grammatical reasons rather than due to the actual spelling of words, which typically come out all jumbled-up) whenever I tried to translate the text automatically into English. Okay, all that said, some of the following plot details may be garbled or out of sequence somewhat, but I'm pretty sure I got most of the major points fairly correct (as well as interspersing bits of detail—if not the direct wording—from other sources, to provide the wrap-up I've quoted a couple of the more easily legible excerpts verbatim at the end of the second paragraph directly below this one). It'd be nice to learn more specific details about some of the individual scenes and the film's technical aspects (such as SFX, if any), but the pictures we're running go far in giving us an idea of the overall "look" of the film (i.e., cheap, crude and schlocky! [not necessarily bad things]). So here goes...

From what I can gather, this is the basic storyline: A well-educated, distinguished and sophisticated big-city medical practitioner (above-mentioned Dr. Effendi, played by Ramlee) moves to the vicinity of the community of Kpg. (short for *kampung*: "village") Kiambang, there at his newly-founded clinic to introduce and practice more modern forms of medicine for the benefit of the superstitious and backward local yokels. This earns him the disap-

proval of the powerful *dukun* ("shaman") Tok, a "faith healer"—basically, a witch doctor—(according to Google Translate, *dukun* can also be translated as "quack") who considers the mod-minded medico a threat to his livelihood, which comes via exploiting the supernatural for his own profit at the expense of the superstitious populace, whereas Effendi openly speaks out against such antiquated beliefs and opposes them. Prior to the out-of-towner doc setting up his practice locally, the area has been plagued by a supernatural entity—a fierce "tigerman", known as Sitora—one of whose potential victims is a beauteous local maiden named Naemah (played onscreen by the actress known mononymously as Fazliyaton), the daughter of a local merchant named Amin, an old warrior ("*pendekar*") and immigrant to the region who puts no stock in its native superstitions. Tok the *dukun* (who is also a lowdown racketeer) has been holding the threat of attacks by Sitora over their heads in order to extort protection payments from the defiantly realist skeptic Amin and other residents of the *kampung*, who'd better pay up...or else. Because Amin the brave old warrior staunchly refuses to pay off Tok to "protect" them, the latter sics Sitora on the locals, resulting in a series of attacks. Although Amin's followers were successful in fending off and wounding the weretiger, it used

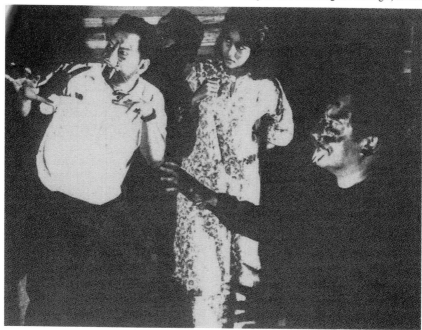

Where Tiger? *There Tiger!* P. Ramlee as the now-monstrified Dr. Effendi (at left), with Sitora, played by Datuk Mahmud June, on the far right. I'm not 100% certain (only about 99.9%), but I'd imagine that the lady in the middle is the actress known as Fazliyaton, playing the film's heroine, Naemah

its magical powers in order to render itself invisible and thus avoid detection/apprehension. Police are notified of the incident. (At least one unverifiable source I saw led me to believe that Tok the sham shaman and Sitora the weretiger might possibly be alter-egos—as in one and the same person in different forms—but I can't say for sure.)

Shortly after his arrival, Effendi hires on Amin's daughter Naemah to function as his nurse, and it isn't long before romance begins to blossom between employer and employee, and eventually their wedding is arranged. The following is taken from the English synopsis I sourced, which continues on from roughly the point where I left off: "Sitora continues his terror. Pendekar Amin, his wife and 3 other warriors are killed. Eventually, Dr. Effendi is attacked by Sitora and he becomes Sitora's designated accomplice to continue the deathly trail of dead bodies whenever he sees himself in the mirror! ...OCPD *[i.e., local law enforcement – ed.]* brings in a more senior doctor from another town, a Dr. Abu Bakar. In spite of being a man of science, his stay in Sarawak had opened his eyes to the possibility of the existence of forces beyond our comprehension. During a trip to Tok Dukun's shack, Dr. Abu Bakar was told that the only way to defeat the demon was with a mystical stick (*kayu tas*)… During the climax, Sitora tricks his new found aide, Dr. Effendi, into kidnapping Naemah and killing her. Just in the nick of time, Dr. Abu Bakar arrives at the scene and saves the day with his own possession of the mystical stick (*kayu tas*) which was presented to him by an Iban headman. Dr. Effendi regains his usual self and sanity is restored in Kpg. Kiambang." And there you have it, for what it's worth…which I hope is a lot, cuz it's all I got!

Although of course the plot of even a film's official tie-in novelization doesn't necessarily always exactly follow that of the film itself in either continuity or specific content, we can only assume that the two bear a more than passing resemblance to one another (at least, you'd think). I'm hoping the above plot breakdown shines at least some interesting light on the dramatic content of the movie. Let's just say that it sure as shit reads more legibly than some of the Malay-to-"English" (note quotes!) translations I looked over and tried to make sense of, but it involved too much guesswork and I didn't want to resort to making too many assumptions and suppositions (although there's definitely a lot of that going on here, nonetheless!). Just for laughs and the sake of comparison, check out this verbatim excerpt from one of said automated (mis) translations: "However, the character of Dr. Afendi [*sic*] was built with one change. Indeed Dr. Afendi [*sic*] is typical Hollywood. Doctors at first did not believe the emergence of a tiger and a leopard

imitation switch invented himself when he himself cursed. And, Dr. Afendi [*sic*] P. Ramlee is an opportunity to tell the story of the mystical exist and not all that mystical nonsense and lies." (Power to that robot translator for at least giving us an inkling though! It does rather amaze me sometimes how these things work, even if they'll likely never be perfect.)

According to one Zaedi Zolkafli in an online posting ("Subject: Malay film Classic", dated March 2013), "**SITORA HARIMAU JADIAN** ('The Tigerman') is said to be lost. But I think the original reel is kept under the dust at some place, unlike the original **PONTIANAK** movies which were literally thrown into the Klang river in Kuala Lumpur. Interesting to note that Music Valley's original catalogue of VCDs has **SITORA HARIMAU JADIAN** (1964), **ORANG LICHIN** (1958) and a few other obscure films but [*sic?*] never got released in the market till now. The list has over 200 titles, which is less than 100% of Malay classic films in official record. Certainly, the company didn't pick up these titles from the air. I hope".

I happened upon a link to an alleged **SITORA HARIMAU JADIAN** VCD from that Music Valley company which Mr. Zolkafli mentioned above (MV is a prolific releaser/distributor of Malaysian movies on disc); although possibly (?) said sparsely-worded listing was merely referring to a CD of the film's soundtrack album, for which a number of songs are still extant. These include two Ramlee duets with his frequent colleague on both celluloid and vinyl—who was also his real-life third wife—the then-rising Singaporean chanteuse Saloma (a.k.a. Primadona Saloma, Salmah binti Ismail or Puan Sri Datin Amar Salmah Ismail, born on January 22, 1935; *Puan Sri* became her official title/status after she and Ramlee—whose own title was *Tan Sri*—were married in 1961.). Entitled *"Mengapa tak berkawan"* and *"Jikalau ku tahu"* (which respectively roughly translate to "Why Not Make Friends" and "If I Knew"), audio rips of these cuts taken from the original 7" 45 rpm vinyl single releases can be found on YouTube, but from the sounds of them they are merely generic commercial pop songs with little or no direct connection to the monster movie in which they appeared (so you can forget hearing any monstrous tiger roars or other horror elements in the mix, cuz it ain't happening!). Interestingly enough, on the **SITORA** soundtrack, the singing voice of songstress Saloma was dubbed over and lip-synched by Fazliyatun, the actress who appeared in the film as its harried heroine Naemah. Incidentally, according to legend, the mononymous Saloma had her stage-name chosen for her by no less than Shaw Bros. big boss Run Run Shaw, who took it from the title character of William Dieterle's 1953 Hollywood biblical epic **SALOME**, starring Rita Hayworth. Saloma was hugely popular as a pop singer, as well as an actress, and was also a major influence on women's hair and fashion trends in some parts of the Eastern Hemisphere. In 1978, she was elected Biduanita Pertama Negara (*"First National Songbird"*) in her country of birth. After her husband Mr. Ramlee died, Saloma became increasingly despondent and depressed, whereafter her health began to deteriorate, and she succumbed to yellow fever at the age of only 48 on April 25, 1983. She was interred alongside the grave of her husband at the Jalan Ampang Muslim Cemetery in Kuala Lumpur.

According to reports, at the time of its original release **SITORA** was as good as disowned by Shaw bigwigs, and it also came under negative scrutiny from Malaysian censors (and presumably religious groups?) due to its open exploitation of and sensationalism regarding its supernatural content. I've only read hints and bits of rumors here and there, but either of these reasons—possibly even a combination of both—might at least in some part explain why the film was not only unceremoniously yanked from circulation, but actually purposely destroyed by interested (or perhaps simply *dis*interested) parties. For all I know, maybe its producers merely thought it was an unmitigated piece of crap, an embarrassment, hence its intentional "disappearance" (the rights to certain of their ex-star Ramlee's films still fall under ownership of the Shaw Bros., not Malaysia's own National Archives, and considering certain Shaws' reps' unfavorable initial reactions to **SITORA** upon its completion, maybe that might well factor in somewhere here too). According to a 2012 posting at the 'blog of Farouk Gulsara (see URL address below), more than one Ramlee film drew negative attention from the local censor board, including his comedic drama **MINTA NOMBOR EKOR** (196?), which was banned due to its depiction of onscreen gambling, including such "shocking" activities as making book on horseracing and playing the lottery. Also banned was his Merdeka-produced romantic drama **GELORA** (1970), this time for sexually suggestive adult content (he also made a 1961 film of the same title, but I am unsure if it too attracted undue censorial attention). So in a morally sensitive climate such as then existed— and still endures, to some extent in Singapore and Malaysia—who knows what lengths certain people might go to in order to prevent certain films from being shown?

I hope I haven't read too much into things here, so I hope you won't too, but by all means read between the lines if you want to…just not too much! Much of what I've given here are verifiable facts,

but quite a bit of it is purely hypothetical as well as hearsay which would never hold up in a court of law. I'm sure that probably reams have been written about this "mystery movie" by Asian writers, but I'd be interested to hear about any reliable English sources I may have overlooked which might help shed further light on things.

NOTES: When I attempted to translate the film's original Malay title using several different automated translators online, the results varied wildly, strangely enough sometimes even within the very same paragraph (e.g., "Tigers Sitora Mutant", "Tora the Tiger's Children" and "Sitora Tiger Imitation"!). My Indonesian sister-in-law Henie Fenton, who is fluent in both Malay and her native language as well as English, had no idea what to make of the title when I asked her to translate it for me (although I think perhaps the unfamiliar proper noun "Sitora" may have thrown her off somewhat). For further info, see "The Lost Were-Tiger!" by Farouk Gulsara (*http://asokan63.blogspot. ca/2012/09/the-lost-were-tiger.html*)

SITORA HARIMAU JADIAN
(*"Sitora the Weretiger"*)
Malaysia, 1964 [Language: Bahasa Melayu]
Director, Screenplay & Music: Tan Sri P. Ramlee
Cast: Tan Sri P. Ramlee (Dr. Effendi), Datuk Mahmud June, Rosmawati, Ali Rahman, Hashim Minah, Fazliyaton
Distributed by the Shaw Organization

Modern poster design by "AlienBiru", found online at DeviantArt (@ *alienbiru. deviantart.com*)

BAKENEKO (化け猫) & *KAIBYŌ* (怪猫) *EIGA* – A SELECT FILMOGRAPHY

Compiled by Steve Fenton (with more than a little help from pre-existing resources!)

*[Where available, video companies are listed at the ends of entries, italicized and in square parentheses; most of the relatively few titles released on DVD have apparently since gone OOP, but copies may still be available via Amazon or eBay (etc). Simply because I'm more interested in the older material in this popular Japanese kaidan-eiga horror subgenre, I have concentrated on more vintage (i.e., mostly pre-1970) titles; but that isn't to say we can't do an addendum to expand it and bring things more up to date in a future issue. Titles are listed in roughly chronological order, by year. The bolded English titles given in all-caps are not necessarily legitimate release titles, but sometimes only loose translations; although a number of those given are in quite popular usage.]

Silent Films:-

San'nō no bakeneko (山王化猫, 1914) – D: Shōzō Makino

LEGEND OF THE GHOST-CAT OF ARIMA (*Arima kaibyō-den*, 1914) – D: ???

THE CAT OF OKAZAKI (*Okazaki no neko*, 1914) – D: Shōzō Makino

NABESHIMA GHOST-CAT (*Nabeshima kaibyō*, 1917) – D: ???

GHOST-CAT OF SAGA (*Saga no bakeneko*, 1916) – D: ???

Akakabe myōjin kaibyō kidan (1918) – D: ???

OKAZAKI GHOST-CAT PASS [*sic?*] (岡崎怪猫伝 / *Ōkazaki kaibyō-den*, 1919) – D: ???

Arima no neko arima kaibyō-den (1920) – D: ???

Hida no kaibyō (1920) – D: ???

LEGEND OF THE NABESHIMA GHOST-CAT (*Nabeshima kaibyō-den*, 1929) – D: Shiroku Nagao

CAT GHOST AND CHERRY BLOSSOMS AT NIGHT IN SAGA (*Kaibyō Saga no yozakura*, 1930) – D: Minoru Ishiyama

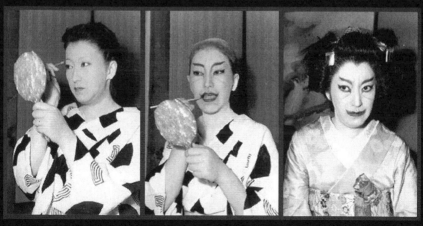

Frequent *kaibyō* actress Takako Irie applies her kabuki-style "ghost-cat" makeup behind-the-scenes on the set of **GHOST-CAT OF ARIMA PALACE** (1953)

Sound Films:-

LEGEND OF THE SAGA CAT MONSTER (佐賀怪猫伝 / *Saga kaibyō-den*, 1931) – D: Shigeru Mokudo

ARIMA CAT UPHEAVAL (*Arima neko sōdō*, 1936) – D: Saitō Hakkō

Poster for **GHOST-CAT OF THE KAR-AKURI TENJO** (1958)

YAJI & KITA'S CAT TROUBLE (*Yaji Kita Okazaki neko taiji*, 1937) – D: Masao Yoshimura

GHOST-CAT OF ARIMA (*Kaidan arima neko*, 1937) – D: Shigeru Mokudo

GHOST-CAT'S MYSTERIOUS SHAMISEN (怪猫謎の三味線 / *Kaibyō nazo no shamisen* a.k.a. *Onshū nazo no kaibyō*, 1938) – D: Kiyohiko Ushihara

GHOST-CAT AND THE RED WALL (怪猫赤壁大明神 / *Kaibyō akakabe daimyojin*, 1938) – D: Kazuo Mori

GHOST-CAT OF GOJUSAN-TSUGI a.k.a. **CAT-GHOST OF THE FIFTY-THREE STATIONS** (怪猫五十三次 / *Kaibyō gojūsan-tsugi*, 1938) – D: Shichinosuke Oshimoto

GHOST-CAT LEGEND (*Kaibyō-den*, 1938) – D: Kanji Suganuma

SILVER CAT'S CURSE (*Noroi no ginbyō*, 1939) – D: Kanenori Yamada

SPIRIT OF THE CAT (*Shinrei jakuneko*, 1940) – D: Ryohei Arai

CAT OF THE YELLOW ROSE (山吹猫 / *Yamabuki neko*, 1940) – D: Tadashi Fujiwara

GHOST-CAT OIL HELL (*Kaibyō abura jigoku*, 1940) – D: Sōya Kumagai

GHOST-CAT OF NABESHIMA (鍋島怪猫伝 / *Nabeshima kaibyōden*, 1949) – D: Kunio Watanabe

GHOST OF SAGA MANSION (怪談佐賀屋敷 / *Kaidan Saga yashiki*, 1953) – D: Ryohei Arai *[Kadokawa Video]*

GHOST-CAT OF ARIMA PALACE (怪猫有馬御殿 / *Kaibyō Arima goten*, 1953) – D: Ryohei Arai

GHOST-CAT OF THE OKAZAKI UPHEAVAL a.k.a. **TERRIBLE GHOST-CAT OF OKAZAKI** (怪猫岡崎騒動英題 / *Kaibyō Okazaki sōdō*, 1954) – D: Bin Kado *[Kadokawa Video]*

WEAK-KNEED FROM FEAR OF GHOST-CAT (怪猫胆怯大騒動 怪猫腰抜け大騒動 / *Kaibyō koshinuke daisodo*, 1954) – D: Torajirō Saitō

GHOST-CAT OF OUMA CROSSING a.k.a. **CAT MONSTER OF OUMA CROSSING** (怪猫逢魔ヶ辻 / *Kaibyō Oumagatsuji*, 1954) – D: Bin Kado *[Kadokawa Video]*

GHOST-CAT OF GOJUSAN-TSUGI a.k.a. **CAT-GHOST OF THE FIFTY-THREE STA-**

...TIONS (怪猫五十三次 / *Kaibyō gojūsan-tsugi*, 1956) – D: Bin Kado *[Kadokawa Video]*

MANY GHOST CATS (怪猫乱舞 / *Kaibyō ranbu*, a.k.a. **THE PHANTOM CAT**, 1956) – D: Masamitsu Igayama

GHOST-CAT OF YONAKI SWAMP a.k.a. **NECROMANCY** (*Kaibyō Yonaki numa*, 1957) – D: Katsuhiko Tasaka *[Kadokawa Video]*

BLACK CAT MANSION a.k.a. **THE MANSION OF THE GHOST-CAT** (亡霊怪猫屋敷 / *Bōrei kaibyō yashiki*, 1958) – D: Nobuo Nakagawa *[Beam Entertainment]*

GHOST-CAT OF THE KARAKURI TENJO a.k.a. **UNCANNY CAT IN THE CEILING** (怪猫からくり天井 / *Kaibyō Karakuri tenjō*, 1958) – D: Kinnosuke Fukuda

GHOST-CAT OF THE CURSED WALL a.k.a. **THE GHOST-CAT CURSED WALL** (怪猫呪いの壁 / *Kaibyō noroi no kabe*, 1958) – D: Kenji Misumi *[Kadokawa Video]*

THE GHOST-CAT OF OTAMA POND (怪奇幻影傑作撰 怪猫 お玉が池 / *Kaibyō Otama-ga-ike*, 1960) – D: Yoshihiro Ishikawa *[Beam Entertainment]*

KURONEKO a.k.a. **THE BLACK CAT** (藪の中の黒猫 / *Yabu no naka no kuroneko*, 1968) – D: Kaneto Shindō *[Criterion & Eureka!]*

THE GHOST-CAT CURSED POND a.k.a. **BAKENEKO: A VENGEFUL SPIRIT** a.k.a. **CAT MONSTER OF THE CURSED LAKE** (*Kaibyō nori no numa*, 1968) – D: Yoshihiro Ishikawa *[Toei Video]*

THE HAUNTED CASTLE (秘録怪猫伝 / *Hiroku kaibyō-den*, 1969) – D: Tokuzō Tanaka *[Kadokawa Video]*

NOTES: I found a goodly chunk of this filmography at a Russian site called Кайданы в кино (*kaidan.org*), especially at the URL addy *http://kaidan.org/bakeneko.html*; then I added to it and padded things out with other titles I found at various other places through Google, cross-referencing whatever I could at the IMDb and elsewhere. I also found some useful info at the German website Kongulas Pranke, subtitled "Monstercon – Monstrula – Vintage Monsters – Prank". It's all in German, but if you right click and auto-translate it into English, it is easily understandable... German *is* the sister tongue of English, after all! (visit *http://www.affengigant.de/kongulaspranke/viewtopic. php?t=5345*). Paghat the Ratgirl's reviews at Weird Wild Realm (*http://www.weirdwildrealm.com/f-hauntedcastle. html*) were also a great help in my research. Tracking down the titles in their original *kanji/hiragana/katakana* characters was a different matter altogether though! I had to dig those up online wherever I could find them; hence, a number of films given here come without their original Japanese titles, because they are so obscure and/or lost that very little information is available on them. It'd take a better Googler than me to deep-search 'em out! *Monster!*'s Facebook friend John Vellutini kindly provided us with a link to a Canadian 'blog called The Horror Cats (*horrorcats.blogspot. ca*), "A Celebration of Felines in Horror Movies and Television"; so by all means give it a browse. Another useful resource was Sci Fi Japan (*www.scifijapan.com*).

Poster for **THE GHOST-CAT CURSED POND** (1968)

NIGHTMARES IN LATEX:
REMEMBERING DON POST MASKS

By John Harrison

FRANKENSTEIN MASK
$16.80 Doz.

To any Monster Kids who grew-up in the 1960s and '70s, the name Don Post was pretty much the only one that counted when it came to high-quality monster masks. While Topstone produced a range of crude but colorful and luridly gaudy rubber masks, and Ben Cooper offered iconic but cheaply-crafted Halloween costumes, Don Post's latex wonders brought an automatic prestige with them, and they became as integral a part of the monster movie craze as Zacherley, *Famous Monsters of Filmland* magazine, Aurora model kits, *The Addams Family* and *The Munsters*, and 8mm Castle Films home movie digests. And yet, because of their comparatively high price tag (especially the masks in their Deluxe range), they were usually out of reach of most Monster Kids, who considered ownership of them as something of a holy grail, and had to content themselves with drooling over the full-page advertisements for them in the back pages of *Famous Monsters*.

Located in Glendale, California, Don Post founded his studios in 1939, selling early latex masks of animals, clowns and other eccentric or amusing characters, before really finding his niche in 1948, when he signed a deal with Universal Studios to produce a mask based on the likeness of Glenn Strange's Frankenstein monster. An instant hit with the kiddies—and no doubt a few cheeky adults, too—Post's Frankenstein mask remained in production for over 25 years, and would have to be considered one of the earliest pieces of monster merchandise, as well as predating the real monster craze by a full decade. Post's

reputation for quality and likeness also saw him working on film productions like the 1956 classic **INVASION OF THE BODY SNATCHERS** (for which he created the giant space pods as well as the human replicas). Don Post Jr. helped broaden the range of masks in the early '70s, and continued running the family business after his father's death in 1979, until the studios finally closed their doors in 2012, putting a full-stop on a classic era of monster fandom after a remarkable run of success and accomplishment.

The most desirable and infamous Don Post masks

Don Post

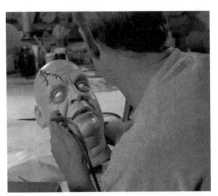

Using an airbrush, a modern-day Post employee (circa early-2000s) applies the finishing touches to a Tor Johnson "Lobo" mask, one of the company's perennial bestsellers

to Monster Kids are the dirty dozen known as the "calendar masks", so dubbed because stunning color portraits of each mask were used in the 1966 Monster Calendar, which was sold at novelty stores and through magazine ads. These were the Deluxe Series of masks, comprising The Wolfman, The Hunchback, The Mummy, The Phantom, The Mole People, Dracula, The Frankenstein Monster, The Metaluna Mutant, The Gorilla, Ygor, The Creature and The Mad Doctor. Spectacular and striking, and sculpted for the most part by the masterful Verne Langdon (who came in to work with Post in 1963), these masks were as beautiful and artfully

crafted as any Aurora box art by James Bama or Basil Gogos cover painting for *Famous Monsters*. A 1965 episode of the wartime sitcom *McHale's Navy* ("The Vampire of Taratupa") featured a guest appearance from The Phantom of the Opera, The Wolfman, The Hunchback and The Mummy, all courtesy of the Don Post calendar masks. Priced around $35 at the time (pairs of hands were around $17), this series of masks were certainly at the high end of monster memorabilia at the time, perhaps the equivalent of today's Hot Toys and Sideshow Premium action figures. In 1998, Don Post Studios reissued the calendar masks in a limited edition, which sold out quickly and began demanding collectors' prices almost immediately.

Like many others of my generation, I first became aware of Don Post masks through *Famous Monsters*, whose editor Forrest J. Ackerman and publisher James Warren clearly had a close association with the studio, as Post produced exclusive masks of Uncle Creepy and Cousin Eerie, the two mascots for Warren's great black and white horror comic magazines *Creepy* and *Eerie*. But Post also offered a whole range of weird, wonderful and ghoulish characters outside of the realm of the classic Universal monsters. There was the perennially favorite Tor Johnson mask, The Fly, Sargoth (a spectacular cobra design), the Rondo Hatton-inspired Mongo mask, and a myriad other assortment of creatures, beasts, crazies and aliens. Post also obtained prestige rights to produce quality masks based on popular current movies and television shows like *The Munsters*, *Star Trek*, *Planet of the Apes* and **STAR WARS**, and of course it was a Don Post William

McHale's Navy episode "The Vampire of Taratupa" featured guest appearances from The Phantom of the Opera, The Wolfman, The Hunchback and The Mummy

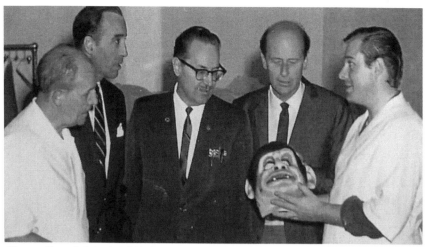

Above: [from left to right] Unidentified, Christopher Lee, Forrest J. Ackerman, Ray Harryhausen and Post's business partner Verne Langdon, in the workshop at Don Post Studios in Glendale, CA, circa the mid/late-'60s

Shatner mask which was famously chosen by John Carpenter for Michael Myers to hide behind in **HALLOWEEN** (1978, USA). Post Studios later worked in an official capacity on the *Halloween* franchise, creating the masks for, and having their factory featured in, 1982's **HALLOWEEN III: SEASON OF THE WITCH** (see review on p. 21). I grew up in the Australia of the 1970s, when finding any cool monster memorabilia was still something of a challenge. The first monster mask I ever obtained was a grey vinyl Frankenstein monster, which I saw sitting in the window of a local hardware/general store in 1978. I had gone down there initially to buy a new fishing reel which I had been saving up my pocket money and doing odd jobs for. But as soon as I spotted that

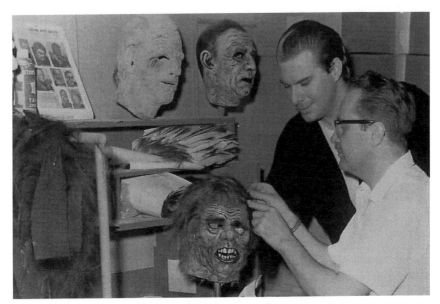

Verne Langdon and Forry Ackerman look over a mask of Quasimodo the hunchback, modeled after the Bud Westmore makeup worn by James Cagney in his title role as Lon Chaney, Sr. in the Hollywood biopic, **MAN OF A THOUSAND FACES** (1957)

mask, all thoughts of casting for trout or redfin disappeared in favor of scaring my friends and the neighborhood kids out of their wits. I snapped up the mask, certain my parents would shake their heads at me for wasting $12 on such an item. It wasn't a Don Post mask, not by any stretch of the imagination, but it was one of my first pieces of monster memorabilia, and the first mask I'd ever owned that didn't come out of a cheap show-bag or off the back of a cereal box (some years later, that Frankenstein mask would meet its demise when I cut it up to make a Leatherface mask to wear to a late-night screening of **THE TEXAS CHAINSAW MASSACRE**).

It wasn't until my first family vacation to the USA, in May of 1980, that I laid hands on a genuine Don Post mask. Ironically, in the end it wasn't a latex monster mask that I bought, but the plastic two-piece Darth Vader helmet, which I purchased at the Disneyland magic shop (at the time, I remember thinking how strange it was that Disneyland was selling **STAR WARS** merchandise. 35 years later, it makes perfect sense!). Why did I choose the Darth Vader mask? Simple…It was the only Don Post mask I came across during my entire vacation, much to my disappointment. I mean, I enjoyed **STAR WARS**, and America at the time was in the grip of **EMPIRE STRIKES BACK** fever, but I was really hoping to return to Australia with a cool Creature or Phantom of the Opera

mask, to put on display in the burgeoning monster museum that was my bungalow bedroom. Even the Universal Studios gift shop proved to be a fizzler. It seemed as if the golden days of monster movie memorabilia had passed me by, and I was caught up in an age of sci-fi hysteria (I liked space adventure, but not as much as I loved being scared by grotesqueries).

My second vacation to America, early the following year, yielded a better result, when I found the Don Post glow-in-the-dark Gargoyle mask at a shop I stumbled across in San Francisco called The Intergalactic Starport, a little store in an arcade near Fisherman's Wharf which specialized in sci-fi/horror/fantasy film memorabilia. I came away from my first of only two visits to that shop with a handful of stills from **ALIEN** and **SUPERMAN: THE MOVIE**, the **DAWN OF THE DEAD** soundtrack LP and a couple of back issues of *Starlog*, but it was the Gargoyle mask that excited me the most. After breaking off with my family to see an early evening screening of **FLASH GORDON**, I returned to the motel room later that night and studied the mask carefully. I can still recall the smell of the thick black vinyl which it was made of (standard for their glow masks, which had the glow material sponge-painted onto the vinyl). Sculpted by future film director Bill Malone and first issued in 1978, the Gargoyle was supposedly inspired by the Haunted Mansion attraction at Disneyland, and had a pretty cool look to him, with elements of the Creature from the Black Lagoon and the Martian monster from **IT! THE TERROR FROM BEYOND SPACE** visible in its design, and a long row of menacing sharp teeth peering out from its wicked grin. The glow effect was bold and effective, and I love that it had a care tag attached, advising the owner how to properly look after their mask for maximum longevity. Unfortunately, I only got to enjoy that Gargoyle mask for a couple of years. The last time I saw it, it was being worn by a school classmate while he rode off down the street on his bike, promising to return it after wearing it to a party that evening (I quickly learned my lesson about lending things to my punk friends!).

As I started earning a bit of mad money through my after-school supermarket job, I ended up buying a variety of different monster masks, including a few more Don Posts which I ordered through *Famous Monsters* during its dying days. I raced home from school every night for weeks for those packages to make their way from Captain Company in New York to the Australian suburb of St. Kilda. But I never really got obsessively into mask collecting—it was an expensive hobby, and the limited lifespan which many of them seemed to have made me wary of accumulating too many. I would have loved the limited Don Post Facehugger mask from **ALIEN**, which came in a plexiglass display case, but its $500 price-tag put it just a little out of reach to a 15-year-old at the time (there was also a stunning limited edition Klaus Kinski mask and hand set from the 1979 Herzog remake of **NOSFERATU**, which originally sold for $300). I decided to stick to collecting monster toys and related paper products that I could preserve and learn from, like magazines, comics, posters, stills and lobby cards. I kept my surviving monster masks for drunken parties and scaring my nieces and nephews whenever they came to visit.

But that was the great thing about Don Post masks, and why their legacy and fan following remains so strong: you didn't always need to actually own them to be inspired by them, to appreciate their artistry, or to have them fire your imagination. But whenever you did get to pull one over your head, a Don Post mask would almost take hold of you, and let the monster in you come alive.

In September of 2014, Blacksparrow Auctions published *The Illustrated History of Don Post Studios* by Lee Lambert, which at nearly 500 pages looks to be the definitive word on the subject, and an essential read for any mask fans and Monster Kids of the period. You can also search YouTube for "Monsterama: History of Don Post Studios", an enjoyable 2004 short featurette hosted by Elvira, which was an episode of her 12-part *Monsterama* series.

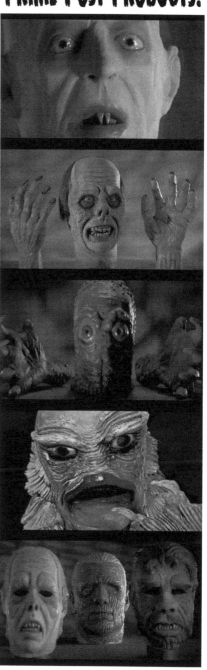

A STUNNING ARRAY OF PRIME POST PRODUCTS!

GHOST STORIES
& MONSTERS:

"THE MONSTER OF DREAD END..."

by Stephen R. Bissette

The sun never shines on Dread End.

Not really.
Not ever.

Under the street that the sun never shines upon, beneath the sidewalks that no human being has tread upon since Dread End was abandoned, there is a whispering of something below, a rustling barely audible from the grates and the drains and the sewers...

Something stirs beneath Dread End.

Something *sinister*. Something *scaly*. Something *hungry*...

The most terrifying monster story of 1962 was not published in a paperback anthology or newsstand science-fiction or mystery pulp or digest. It did not appear in something "presented" by Alfred Hitchcock or Rod Serling, and it was not broadcast on television or unreeling in movie theaters or drive-ins.

The most horrific monster story of 1962 was published in four colors—in a comicbook. It did not appear in a "monster" comicbook, nor was it even published by one of the many publishers (Atlas/Timely, National Periodicals/DC Comics, Charlton Comics, etc.) cranking out a plethora of "monster comics" at a rapid clip that fateful year. "Monster comics," to us kids (I was seven years old at the time), were comicbooks featuring monsters on their covers—including "non-monster" titles like *Detective Comics, Batman, Superman, Action Comics, Tomahawk, Sea Devils, The Brave and the Bold, Showcase*, etc.—as well as truly monster-centric titles like *Tales of the Unexpected, Mysterious Suspense, House of Mystery, House of Secrets* (both of which were, at the time, strictly SF-fantasy in nature), *Tales of Suspense, Amazing Fantasy, Tales to Astonish*, "The War That Time Forgot" issues of *Star-Spangled War Stories*, and the new breed of monster comics: *Konga, Gorgo*, and *Kona Monarch of Monster Isle*, among others.

In fact, the most unnerving monster story of 1962 was published by a publisher whose "Pledge to Parents" had less than a decade earlier promised concerned parents everywhere that their strict policies and devotion to higher editorial principles "eliminates, rather than regulates, objectionable material", concluding their vow with the memorable mantra, "Dell Comics Are Good Comics".

How, then, could it be that Dell Comics published the most deranged, demented, and delicious monster story of 1962, "The Monster of Dread End..."?

Furthermore, how was it that such a tale was told by the prolific writer of the beloved *Marge's Little Lulu* comic series, and illustrated by the artist whose work dated back to Golden Age titles like *Boy Comics, Joker Comics*, and *Romantic Western*?

Let's lift the manhole cover, and see what lies beneath...

————

Before "The Monster of Dread End...," there was *The World Around Us* comicbook series from the publishers of *Classics Illustrated*, and its 24th issue, *The Illustrated Story of Ghosts* (cover-dated August, 1960). Though it remains among the most neglected and forgotten of all four-color horror comicbooks, it was arguably among the most important of its day simply because it existed and was sold on American newsstands across the country—apparently without controversy.

The atmospheric cover seems absolutely tepid by 21st Century standards, but to see such a chilling cover image in 1960 was a novelty indeed. Four-color horror comicbooks had been purged completely from the newsstands half-a-decade earlier by the institution of the self-regulatory Comics Code Association—but here was a painted image of a dilapidated mansion precariously perched on a crumbling protrusion of land under a full yellow disc of a moon, which was spotlighting the uppermost and largest of a flurry of bats flapping up from the rear of the building. Superimposed over this painting was a spectral white-line delineation of a cowled Death figure, its face (if it had a face) lost in shadow, pointing one finger directly at the viewer/reader, the other pointing back at a crudely-painted "Rooms for Rent" sign tilting before the rotting building.

A more classical ghost-and-haunted-house image would be hard to imagine, and this one—an open challenge to the reader, a dare not to rent a room but rather to touch the comic itself and turn to the first page—was a complete anomaly on the 1960 newsstands. Weren't horror comics a thing of the past?

And why, pray tell, would *Classics Illustrated* be the one publisher placing such a cover on the newsstands? Weren't they *above* this sort of thing?

What was forgotten, had it ever been noticed or known at all outside of the comicbook industry itself, was the fact that *Classics Illustrated* had *never stopped publishing horror comicbooks*. They had kept almost all their genre novel adaptations—Mary Shelley's *Frankenstein*, Robert

CLASSICS Illustrated — FRANKENSTEIN

MARY W SHELLEY

Featuring Stories by the World's Greatest Authors

No. 26 15¢

Cover art for the 1960s reprint of *Classics Illustrated #26, Frankenstein*, cover art by the late great Norman Saunders. Shortly after painting this cover, Saunders indelibly marked the decade with his trading card art for Topps, particularly for the infamous *Mars Attacks!* cards

Louis Stevenson's *Dr. Jekyll and Mr. Hyde*, Victor Hugo's *The Hunchback of Notre Dame*, etc.—essentially in print and available by mail-order and periodic reissues without noticeable lapses.

Classics Illustrated were one of only two American four-color newsstand comicbook publishers who had refused to participate in the self-regulation of the industry, who stood apart from the formation of the Comics Code Authority in 1954-55, and who never once published a comicbook with the CCA "Seal of Approval" blemishing their cover art.

The distributors and retailers who were so vigilant after 1955 in racking only those comicbooks emblazoned with the CCA Seal never hesitated to continue racking *Classics Illustrated*. After all, despite the handful of *Classics Illustrated* that had been cited in the various angry editorials, articles, books, radio, and television attacks about/upon the comicbook industry, and in spite of those critics (Dr. Fredric Wertham prominent among them) who claimed that the mere act of

adapting great literature to the comics medium was inherently debasing—of the literature, and the readers—*Classics Illustrated* rode the storm successfully and without lasting stigma. Even the rare citations of specifically "objectionable" *Classics Illustrated* cover art or images in the state and the Federal Senate Subcommittee investigation of the comicbook industry had failed to stain the publisher's reputation. *Classics Illustrated* did quietly "retire" some targeted titles for a time, make editorial alterations to some covers, and even completely revise the text and art to certain issues (*Dr. Jekyll and Mr. Hyde* and *The Hunchback of Notre Dame* prominent among them), but they continued publishing without too many ruffled feathers. *Classics Illustrated* were, by 1955, an accepted institution and imprint, and rode that reputation past the blistering scourge of the industry at large into ongoing success into the 1960s (more on this below).

Thus, they were *almost* alone among the surviving comicbook publishers who might still dare to publish such a cover, and to make such a dare to readers.

"Enter, if you dare", the cover art by Norman Nodel clearly asserted, without a word. The pointing spectre spoke volumes, and the effective graphics surrounding that image (particularly the similarly white-overlay lettering of the oversized word "GHOSTS") functioned as a calling card to two classes of comicbook readers: those who had once loved and sorely missed the horror comicbooks of the early 1950s, and those (like me) who had never laid eyes on a comicbook that hinted at such a resurrection.

Mind you, there was *one* other publisher who *could* have dared, but wouldn't—until two years later. In a way, the success of and lack of outrage over *The Illustrated Story of Ghosts* arguably led to the publication of "The Monster of Dread End..."

The World Around Us was, as the indicia claimed, "published monthly by Gilberton World-Wide Publications, Inc." of New York City. In an era when comics for the most part never included credits for their contents, Gilberton was among those (like Dell) whose indicia habitually cited key company personnel, namely in the case of *The World Around Us* series Executive Editor Meyer A. Kaplan, series editor Roberta Strauss Feuerlicht, and art director Leonard B. Cole, a.k.a. L.B. Cole.

Remember that latter name, please, if you remember no other for the next couple of pages.

The *World Around Us* series was among Gilberton's experimental expansion of their line in the 1950s and early 1960s. Beginning in 1951, founder and publisher Albert Kanter was certain enough of the stability of the *Classics Illustrated* line (with over 100 adaptations/issues published, and most of them enjoying multiple revisions and/or print runs) to begin developing new titles and series. All adhered to the educational imperative of Kanter's agenda, beginning with two modest corporate-sponsored 16-page one-shots, *Shelter Through the Ages* (1951, sponsored by Rubberoid) and the self-descriptive *The Westinghouse Story: The Dreams of Man* (1953), both illustrated by Harry C. Kiefer. Kiefer had in fact defined the house style of the imprint in the late 1940s, including the occasionally horrific graphic adaptations of *The Hunchback of Notre Dame* (*Classics Illustrated* #18, April-June 1949), *The Adventures of Sherlock Holmes* (#33, January 1947), *Great Expectations* (#43, November 1947), *Mysteries of Paris* (#44, December 1947), and *Wuthering Heights* (#59, May 1949), along with the ghost-populated *A Christmas Carol* (#53, November 1948) and the indelibly grotesque sailors-vs.-cephalopod sequence in *20,000 Leagues Under the Sea* (#47, May 1948). Axes were wielded and octopus gore splashed the deck of Captain Nemo's Nautilus in every edition I ever beheld in my lifetime.

Following the two one-shots, Kanter debuted the short-lived *Picture Progress* educational comics series, which was specifically packaged for schools (18 issues, 1953-55). The more child-friendly fairy tale series *Classics Illustrated Junior* also launched in the fall of 1953, proving far more successful as an essentially monthly series specifically designed for younger readers (1953-62). The more adult-oriented 35-cent *Classics Illustrated Special Issues* debuted with the ambitious 96-page *The Story of Jesus* (December 1955), expanding into handsome squarebound comic-format specials on history, science, war, industry, and religion (1955-62, including a World's Fair Special Issue in 1964 that was not published or distributed in America).

Building on that success, the 25-cent monthly *The World Around Us* series debuted with the 80-page *The Illustrated Story of Dogs* (#W1, September 1958). Ever-eclectic in scope, subject matter, and art styles (each issue featured individual stories and/or chapters drawn by a different artist or art team), the series cut back its page count to 72 pages with one of its most successful issues, *The Illustrated Story of Prehistoric Animals* (#W15, November 1959).[1] Hitting newsstands at the

THE ILLUSTRATED STORY OF **GHOSTS**

Splash page for *The World Around Us #24, The Illustrated Story of Ghosts* (1960; hereafter *Ghosts* in subsequent captions); art by EC Comics veteran George Evans. This Halloween-friendly image also seemed to hint that maybe, just maybe, the EC Old Witch was coming back...?

height of the late-1950s/early 1960s dinosaur boom, that particular issue of *The World Around Us* hit real paydirt.

Classics Illustrated scholar William B. Jones, Jr. has authored the definitive reference book on the publisher—in two editions, no less—and with his kind indulgence, let's savor his insights on *The Illustrated Story of Ghosts*:

> "*Ghosts* was something of a departure for

---

1 I cannot neglect to mention that this is the first comicbook

I remember being purchased for me, at my request, when I was only four years old. I wore out the first copy, but so adored the comic that my mother took the rare-in-1959 step of buying me a second copy; an act of love I will never forget or be able to repay. Studiously reading and rereading every page, and specifically copying the pages drawn by artists Sam Glanzman and Al Williamson, I can trace my desire to draw my own comics back to this comicbook—so, you could say that I owe my comics career to *The World Around Us*!

Left: George Evans art, "The Hitch-Hiker" from *Ghosts* (1960): Evans was a master of mood, offering a definitive comics telling of this famous urban legend. **Right:** Gray Morrow art, "Room for the Night" from *Ghosts* (1960): Variations of this urban legend had already appeared in pulps, radio, comics, and in film, notably the Orson Welles/Hilton Edwards Academy-Award-nominated short film *Return To Glennascaul* (a.k.a. *Orson Welles' Ghost Story,* 1951/53)

The World Around Us, which, even in its lighter moments, had focused only upon the factual and verifiable. Although some attention was given to research on extrasensory perception, most of the book was just plain fun. The best sections were the modern urban myths "The Hitch-Hiker", strikingly rendered by George Evans, and "Room for the Night", superbly drawn by Gray Morrow. Both Evans and Morrow understood the atmospheric imperatives of the tales they were recreating, and their rain-soaked, cross-hatched panels exude a delicious creepiness."[2]

A departure it was indeed, as was its immediate

successor, *The Illustrated Story of Magic* (#W25, September 1960), which boasted more fine work from Evans, Morrow, Norman Nodel, George Peltz, and others. But *Magic* wasn't as outré in the context of *The World Around Us* series. "Delicious creepiness" neatly sums up *Ghosts,* especially in the horror comicbook desert of 1960. I was five years old when this appeared on comic racks, and I'd never seen anything like it in my wee little life.

There was no outcry from concerned parents or educators. *Ghosts* and *Magic* never provoked controversy of any kind. To verify this, I asked *Classics Illustrated* expert William Jones, Jr. directly about the matter, and he replied,

"The content of the two *WAU* books was never an issue. By the time Gilberton's *Ghosts* (WAU 24) and *Magic* (WAU 25) appeared in August-September 1960, the hysterical phase of the anti-comics crusade had

2 William B. Jones, Jr., *Classics Illustrated: A Cultural History, Second Edition* (2011, McFarland & Company, Inc.), pp. 265-266. This section of this article owes a profound debt to Jones' research and both editions of his book (2002 and 2011; the first edition actually saw print in November 2001, but is copyrighted 2002).

spent itself. For more than a year, *Classics Illustrated* had been returning to its active catalogue several discontinued titles that had been censured by legislative bodies or cultural critics in the early- and mid-1950s, including No. 90, *Green Mansions* (January 1959); No. 89, *Crime and Punishment* (September 1959); No. 13, *Dr. Jekyll and Mr. Hyde* (November 1959); No. 28, *Michael Strogoff* (March 1960); No. 36, *Typee* (March 1960); No. 25, *Two Years Before the Mast* (May 1960); and No. 41, *Twenty Years After* (May 1960). Curiously enough, the bloodiest Classics Illustrated title ever, and the one that was most truly a "horror" comic—No. 26, *Frankenstein* (December 1945)—completely escaped Dr. Wertham's or Senator Kefauver's notice and was never dropped from the Gilberton back-cover re-order lists."[3]

Jones is correct in citing the Evans and Morrow entries as the most vividly unnerving of the stories in *Ghosts*—in fact, George Evans' eye-popping splash image of a cackling witch riding a broom in the night sky, surrounded by ghosts, was the first image to greet the eye. It gave hope to those who recognized the iconography in the context of still-fresh comics history: The Old Witch was back, so to speak. Evans, after all, was a veteran of the once-revered-but-infamous EC Comics horror titles *Tales from the Crypt*, *The Haunt of Fear*, and *The Vault of Horror*. Gilberton was a lifesaver for Evans and other former EC artists who, due to their drawing styles and/or circumstances, hadn't made the leap to the magazine-format *Mad* (which, as a black-and-white magazine, didn't have to submit itself to Code scrutiny, and thrived, becoming the best-selling American comics magazine of the 1960s). Any affiliation with EC was a badge of shame to most publishers still active in the field, and Evans, Al Williamson, Angelo Torres, Reed Crandall, and even on-his-

H.J. Kihl art, "The Talking Mongoose" from *Ghosts* (1960): The closest 'thing' to a monster in *Ghosts* was this account of the poltergeist known as Gef, whose story was a favorite of the 1930s British tabloid press

way-out-of-comics-altogether Graham "Ghastly" Ingels found a haven with Gilberton at a time when an EC vet finding *any* work in comics was difficult at best.[4]

Gray Morrow's artwork was very much in the EC style, and he actually did three pieces in *Ghosts*: "Room for the Night", in which a man spends a stormy night in a house that is revealed by light of day to be a long-abandoned ruin; "Ghosts That

---

3 William B. Jones, Jr., replying to my email question(s) on October 20th, 2014; quoted with permission. I am skating over far more complex individual issue histories here; tracking the printings of *Classics Illustrated* is best left to experts like William. Concerning the *Dr. Jekyll and Mr. Hyde* editions, William notes *Jekyll and Hyde* "was in print, with Arnold Hicks's art and Evelyn Goodman's godawful but fun script, from 1943 to 1953. A painted cover by Mort Künstler and new interior art by Lou Cameron, with a more faithful script, were introduced in 1953, but that edition was taken off the reorder list in November 1955. It returned in November 1959 and never went out of print again, becoming one of the best-selling CI titles. So it was available in 1960 and 1962." I would argue the *Classics Illustrated Dr. Jekyll and Mr. Hyde* was the first American horror comicbook (and comics historian/scholar Mike Benton agrees); for more information, see *Classics Illustrated: A Cultural History, Second Edition*, pp.42-43, for discussion of the 1943 Arnold Hicks version of *Dr. Jekyll and Mr. Hyde*, and pp. 145-146 for analysis of the Lou Cameron revision.

4 Among the contributions EC artists made to the *Classics Illustrated* line was the interior artwork for H.G. Wells' *The First Men in the Moon* (#144, May 1958; six printings through to 1969) by George Woodbridge, Al Williamson, Angelo Torres, and Roy Krenkel. H.G. Wells' sf adaptations were enormously popular. Many were horrific in nature: *The War of the Worlds* (#124, January 1955, art by Lou Cameron; eleven printings to 1970), *The Time Machine* (#133, July 1956, art by Lou Cameron; nine printings to 1971), *The Invisible Man* (#153, November 1959, art by Norman Nodel; seven printings to 1971), etc. Pete Von Sholly notes *The War of the Worlds* was a particular favorite for many: "Love those grey tentacle martians—and they were pretty scary at the time!" (Von Sholly, email, October 21st, 2014).

THE WEREWOLF WASP

YOUR LATEST FIND, BOBBY? WHAT IS IT?

A WASP, MOTHER! BUT A VERY UNUSUAL ONE! THERE'S NOTHING IN ANY OF MY INSECT BOOKS THAT LOOKS LIKE HIM!

IT CERTAINLY IS FEROCIOUS LOOKING!

WASPS ARE FEROCIOUS, MOTHER... THEY'RE THE TERRORS OF THE INSECT WORLD!

I CAN'T WAIT TO SHOW THIS TO PRO- FESSOR LARVAY. HE'LL KNOW WHAT IT IS!

HE OUGHT TO-ONE OF THE WORLD'S FORMOST ENTOMOLOGISTS.

FUNNY... IT SEEMS TO GROW LARGER BY THE MINUTE!

Splash page from *Ghost Stories* #1, "The Werewolf Wasp," script by John Stanley, art by Ed Robbins, one of the most curiously nonsensical nightmare tales in this debut issue

Make a Racket", a splash/chapter lead page for the section on poltergeists; and the final one-pager, "A Question of Ghosts," a coda grace-note comprised of a half-dozen verbal puns and slang terms related to the moniker (i.e., ghost writers, ghost towns, etc.). The lush illustrative styles of Morrow and Evans tie the book together nicely, lending credence to the leaner, less-atmospheric storytelling of artists Jack Abel (the western legend of "The Ghost of Gold Gulch", which may have been better served by Evans' hand, but still boasts one of Abel's more lavish comics art jobs), William A. Walsh (the comfortably domestic, almost comical "The House of Flying Objects"), and the non-comic-format George Peltz illustrations gracing the abridged text adaptation of Théophile Gautier's short story "The Mummy's Foot" (originally published in French as "*Le pied de momie*" in 1840). The latter remains a lost opportunity by any measure, but typical of Gilberton's aesthetic preferences: a proper comics adaptation maybe flirted too overtly with vividly depicting severed limbs.

The final pages of the comic were indeed dedicated to ESP, illustrated by John Tartaglione and cover artist Norman Nodel; the concluding pages of Tartaglione's "The Sixth Sense" is a verbatim retelling of E.F. Benson's short story "The Bus Conductor" (1906, originally published in *The Pall Mall Magazine*), related here as "fact". Older readers of the time would have recognized it as Basil Dearden's opening ghost story about the Hearse Driver (Miles Malleson) in **DEAD OF NIGHT** (1945), already a late-night TV fixture by 1960.

My personal favorite in *Ghosts* stuck with me for life. It was the 9-page account of "The Talking Mongoose", the Isle of Man's famed 1930s poltergeist case of Gef, the "speaking mongoose". Delineated effectively by perhaps the weakest artist in the collection, H.J. Kihl—who, according to Jones, was "contributor to 21 of 36 *World Around Us* issues"[5]—this was the sole "creature" story among the ghost stories herein, and as such the most intriguing to me. Gef was an invisible, initially threatening home invader never seen by the family confronted with the noisy, abusive, and surprisingly verbal "thing" living between their walls, floors, and ceilings. A darker companion to the friendly anthropomorphized stop-motion-animated squirrel in George Pal/Irving Pichel's **THE GREAT RUPERT** (1950, which I'd seen as a lad on TV one afternoon), Gef was both appealing and sort of scary—at one point biting someone after inviting them to put their fingers in his mouth—and his remaining unseen, save for a shadow, only added to his spooky allure.

As I grew older I was delighted to find other accounts of the so-called "Dalby Spook" in various pop paperbacks and storybooks about ghosts and the unexplained. Gef had been a tabloid sensation in the UK, in its heyday yielding a book, *The*

5 Jones, *Classics Illustrated: A Cultural History, Second Edition*, pg. 232.

"Always room for one more!": Look familiar, **DEAD OF NIGHT** devotees? John Tartaglione art, "The Sixth Sense" in *Ghosts* (1960)

Haunting of Cashen's Gap: A Modern 'Miracle' Investigated (by Harry Price and Richard Lambert, 1936, Methuen & Co., Ltd.). Nevertheless, it's the *Ghosts* comic telling that introduced me to the case history (however suspect it remains), and Kihl's sketchy, tentative linework appealed to me as a child. It read so clearly; though I never liked Kihl's sole *Classics Illustrated* art job (*Jane Eyre*, CI #39, the 1962 revision) for being too spare and impoverished, his telling of Gef's enigmatic appearance remains a high point of my early horror comics reading experiences.

Until, that is, my first exposure to Dread End.

Frankly, nothing could have prepared me for "The Monster of Dread End..."

I remember being a little confused the first time I laid eyes on the cover to Dell Comics' *Ghost Stories* #1, on a friend's front porch. Hadn't I seen this cover before?

A white-outlined spectral figure, no face visible beneath its cowl, pointing out at me with one finger, and pointing backwards with the other toward a gravestone and a brown dilapidated house—yes, I was sure I'd seen it before. But that wasn't possible: this was a new comicbook, just out, in a stack of brand-new Walt Disney and superhero comicbooks.

Though I had no name for it at the time, this was perhaps my first experience of *déjà vu*.

I had seen this cover before—I couldn't take my eyes off it for a while. It was strangely familiar.

Then, I turned to the inside front cover, which triggered another feeling of *déjà vu*:

I knew this artist's hand, *I knew this drawing style*.

Ghost Stories #1 (1962), "The Black Stallion" page, artwork by Gerald McCann. Note that McCann did all the interior art for Ghost Stories #2-5 (1963-64), though John Stanley no longer wrote the stories.

This only troubled me further; it wasn't a comfort. This was—weird.

Only later would I put it all together: the Ghost Stories #1 cover art was almost identical to that of The World Around Us #W24, The Illustrated Story of Ghosts.

No surprise, really, since L.B. Cole was art director at Gilberton when Ghosts was published—and Cole was subsequently the art director at Dell Comics when Ghost Stories #1 was designed, packaged, and published.

What conclusion can one draw, but that Cole recycled his own cover concept?

When I asked William Jones about this, he replied: "I'm sure the cover swipe was Cole's idea. The [World Around Us] Ghosts cover was painted by Cole's friend Norman Nodel, who was responsible for Cole being hired in 1958 as Gilberton's art director. So, although Cole wasn't the artist who actually did the cover art for WAU 24, it's certainly possible that he suggested to his friend Mr. Nodel something of the theme. In any case, I'm sure that in 1962, the Ghosts cover was still fresh in the Dell art director's mind, and swiping

is a hallowed comics tradition."[6]

As a 30+-year veteran professional comics artist who has often worked with cover editors, I'll take this a step further: the similarities are so close that I'm convinced that Norman Nodel was working from a Cole cover sketch in 1960—and that Cole recycled or redrew that cover sketch for the Dell Ghost Stories cover art in 1962.

But let's go back to my seven-year-old self, puzzling over that Ghost Stories cover:

Furthermore, the artist who drew the inside front-cover story, the inside-back cover piece, and the unsettling final color story, "The Black Stallion", was another Classics Illustrated and The World Around Us alumni, the prolific Gerald McCann.[7] This guy's art was stiff and not particularly appealing to me, but it nevertheless seemed "more real", somehow, than other comic artists' work. McCann's art made me uneasy for some reason, and hence more compelling. It's difficult to articulate why.

Then my eyes drifted over to the first page of the lead story, a rough-hewn depiction of an abandoned wet city neighborhood at night, and life was never the same again.

———

"The Monster of Dread End…" opens with a noir-ish image of a rain-soaked tenement, the street cordoned-off with a chain and an ominous "Keep Out" sign. "Long empty of human life, the dark, decaying tenements of Dread End stare silently across at each other as though still frozen in horror at the memory of the frightful scenes they alone had once been witness to…"

This was followed by the image of a street corner where children are playing, watched over by a policeman. A partially obscured street sign, cut off by the panel border, reads "Play Street", and a blonde pony-tailed girl wearing a red dress is playing jump-rope in the foreground. But the next

6 Jones, email exchange with the author, October 20th, 2014; quoted with permission.

7 William Jones rightfully dedicates an entire chapter of Classics Illustrated: A Cultural History—chapter XX, "Gerald McCann: The Colors of the Sky" (2nd edition, pp. 213-216)— to this artist, whose distinctive dry-brush and split-pen-nib style was unlike any other artist working in comics at the time. I was particularly intrigued and enamored with his artwork for Classics Illustrated #149, Off on a Comet (March 1959), and though I didn't know they were his cover paintings at the time, I also was obsessed with McCann's (unsigned) covers for First Men In the Moon (#144, May 1958) and (signed, but illegible to my eyes at the time) The Food of the Gods (#160, January 1961). The latter remains the best giant chicken cover in comics history, alongside Robert Crumb's for the underground Funny Aminals [sic] (1972).

LONG EMPTY OF HUMAN LIFE, THE DARK, DECAYING TENEMENTS OF **DREAD END** STARE SILENTLY ACROSS AT EACH OTHER AS THOUGH STILL FROZEN IN HORROR AT THE MEMORY OF THE FRIGHTFUL SCENES THEY ALONE HAD ONCE BEEN WITNESS TO...

KEEP OUT

TIME WAS... WHEN DREAD END, THEN KNOWN AS HAWTHORN PLACE, WAS A BUSY, NOISY, HAPPY STREET THAT ECHOED TO THE SOUND OF CHILDREN'S LAUGHTER...

...THEN EARLY ONE MORNING: THE FIRST... ONE... WAS FOUND...

WH-WHAT'S THAT-?

panel shows a milkman stepping out of his truck under an ink-smeared sky, his mouth agape and eyes narrowed: "Wh-what's THAT—?"

A turn of the page reveals not what the milkman saw, but the street scene of fearful adults, hands to their open mouths, in shock at what we can't see. Effectively breaking the cardinal comics rule of "Show, Don't Tell", the caption reads, "...it was a balled-up thing... like an empty wrapper thrown carelessly aside... but somehow still recognizable as having once been human..." And to the far right of the panel, a boy is bolting down ce-

ment stairs, shouting, "HEY! MY KID SISTER IS MISSING! HER BED IS EMPTY—!"

Whoa. This was beyond merely weird. This was already getting under my skin in ways I didn't know comicbook stories could.

What "killed" this street? Why was it abandoned? What happened to that little girl who was playing jump rope? Was she the missing sister?

This was children disappearing—being kidnapped, and *worse*.

Worst of all was the fact I couldn't *see* what the adults in the story were reacting to. The picture that horrid caption put in my mind—"a balled-up thing… like an empty wrapper"—were like the wrapped-up insect mummies we found in spider's webs, or the empty garter snake shed skins we'd sometimes find outdoors. This comic wasn't like the "monster comics" I loved to read. This comic was putting repellent images in my head in ways nothing ever had before. This was—*creepy.*

The slashing ink lines—unsigned artwork I learned decades later was by Ed Robbins, according to what few sources exist for identifying Dell Comics artists—were in and of themselves disturbing, and the story's events only became more alarming. More panicking adults; more children disappearing, the windows to their bedrooms yawning wide; and worse yet, another thing that cannot-be-shown as a woman cries, "POLICE!" ("Outside on the street another balled-up thing was found…"). By the next page, the blacks are blacker, the faces more desperate, the windows being boarded up, only to be ripped to splinters in the next panel as a terrified mother shouts, "THE TWINS ARE GONE!"

This was the scariest thing I'd ever read, and it was just getting started.

What was visible to comicbook readers in 1962 was that something fundamental changed with Dell Comics. Suddenly, some of the titles we'd bought as Dell Comics were no longer Dell Comics—they were Gold Key Comics, and Dell was publishing some really intriguing stuff that we'd never heard of before.

To dinosaur and monster comic-loving little me, this meant that there was some confusion. One of my favorites, *Turok Son of Stone*, had been a Dell Comic all my life. It suddenly changed without really changing: the cover art looked the same, the interior art looked the same, and the stories and backup stories (the glorious all-dinosaur "The Young Earth") were still the same. But now *Turok* was a Gold Key Comic, and the ads in both the Dells and the Gold Keys seemed to be announcing this and that befuddlement. So, no more *Turok* at Dell?

No worries: that very year, Dell launched the most marvelous caveman-and-dinosaur-and-monster comic of all time, *Kona Monarch of Monster Isle*, with the greatest painted dinosaur and monster covers ever (the first issue sported a cover painting by Thomas Beecham), and the interiors were entirely drawn by that "SJG" and "Glanzman" artist I loved so, so, *so* much, ever since *The World Around Us: The Illustrated Story of Prehistoric Animals.*

Hey, this wasn't a bad thing! Now I had *two* caveman-and-dinosaurs-and-monster comics to watch out for!

What we didn't know, and couldn't know, and wouldn't have understood had it even been explained to us, was that Dell had, since shortly after the launch of the Dell Comics line, been publishing comics predominantly packaged by the Western Publishing Company.[8] It was Western that held the lucrative licenses—with Walt Disney (via K.K. Publications, a subsidiary of Western) and Warner Bros. and Whitman (another division of Western) and Edgar Rice Burroughs, Inc. and Roy Rogers and Gene Autry and Walter Lantz Studio and Smokey the Bear and Lassie and all those movie and TV shows and animated cartoons—and put the comics together as comics, working hand-in-glove with Dell's editorial offices in New York. The artists whose work I loved but had no idea of their names, from Carl Barks ("the good duck artist") to Jesse Marsh (*Tarzan*) to Alberto Giolitti (*Turok*), were all working for Western, not for Dell. Dell handled financing, distribution, invoicing, and returns while Western handled securing rights, creating, and printing the comicbooks.

To make a long story short, when Dell started experimenting in the late 1950s with higher cover prices, the long-standing and ever-fruitful collaboration between Western and Dell began to fray. In the wake of the 1955 comicbook market implosion, it was decided that Western and Dell would part company in 1962.

Dell was suddenly left without its most lucrative licenses, titles, and properties—the bedrock of Western's brand-new Gold Key Comics line—and were scrambling to fill monthly schedules in short order with brand-new concepts, characters, and titles. Some of them—like *Turok* and *Kona*—showed Dell imitating what it once had. They did so in hopes of keeping readers and market share by making comics *just like* what they had been publishing with Western.

Other comics, like *Ghost Stories* and its companion *Tales from the Tomb*, were unlike anything Western had ever packaged before.

---

8 The Western Printing and Lithographing Company was based in Racine, Wisconsin, with editorial offices in Los Angeles, California and New York, New York. The Western/ Dell partnership began in 1938.

Dell editor Don Arneson was among those in Dell's New York City offices dealing with the fallout of the split with Western. With Western's new imprint Gold Key Comics about to launch, the pressure was on to compete with the very packager and provider of Dell's hottest-selling properties.

Gone would be Dell's ability to continue publishing solid genre TV-and-movie tie-ins and strong sellers like *The Twilight Zone*, and Western/Gold Key had already latched onto new properties like *Boris Karloff's Thriller* (soon to be *Boris Karloff's Tales of Mystery*, as the comicbook franchise outlived the TV series that spawned it). How to compete with the venerable Movie Comics adaptations under the Dell seal?

Whether it was a conscious acknowledgement of Dell's unusual status as one of only two (now three: Gold Key was Code-proof, too, by proxy) newsstand comicbook publishers free of the regulatory Comics Code Authority or not, the fact is and was that Dell and Code-free Gilberton alone could truly exploit the monster and horror "boom" of 1962. At the time, their lower-profile competitor in Connecticut, Charlton Comics, was unique in competing with Dell by licensing movie adaptations and spin-offs with MGM and with American-International Pictures (hereafter AIP) working within the parameters of the Comics Code's rules. Charlton's titles included AIP's 1962 adventure movie *Marco Polo* (with art by Sam Glanzman), along with the monster comics titles *Konga* (1960, licensed from AIP), *Gorgo* (1961, licensed from the King Brothers and MGM)—both by writer Joe Gill and artist Steve Ditko—and *Reptilicus* (1962, licensed from AIP; changed to *Reptisaurus* with its third issue).

Dell wasn't too worried. They intended to keep their lion's share of the lucrative movie and TV tie-in marketplace—whatever Western/Gold Key wasn't "taking," that is (the dependable Disney titles, adaptation, and franchises all stayed with Western/Gold Key, for example).

Horror and monsters were blazing hot, and with Western about to flood newsstands with Gold Key titles based on Dell's previous bestsellers (*Walt Disney's Comics and Stories, Bugs Bunny, Tarzan of the Apes*, etc.), Dell took everything a step further. They decided to experiment with a potentially risky departure from their Dell Pledge to Parents:

Horror comics!

Under orders from upstairs, editor Don Arneson and art director/editor L.B. Cole met with vet

Little Lulu writer John Stanley to cook up *new* titles, original to Dell and free of licensing constraints. They were thus able to go further into conceptual and commercial territory untapped since the 1954-55 purge of the entire American comicbook industry (with the notable exception of Gilberton's *Classics Illustrated* like *Frankenstein*, which was still in print unchanged from its blood-and-thunder December 1945 edition[9]).

Arneson, Cole, and Stanley were surely walking a tightrope of sorts—how to create a genuinely effective horror comic, without going too far beyond Dell's still-stringent editorial policies?—and were doing so within very tight time and budgetary constraints.

There would be *two* comicbooks published in this experiment, both to hit newsstands in late summer, cover-dated to stay on sale into the Halloween season: a 12-cent 32-pager (36 pages, with covers), and a bigger, bolder 25-cent "Dell Giant" (84 pages, with covers). Stanley would script over 120 pages of original comics material, working with a hastily assembled team of dependable deadline-making artists, with art director L.B. Cole designing both covers (and, by some accounts, painting the cover for *Tales from the Tomb*).[10]

At the same time, Dell's unique non-Code status allowed them to sign with Universal Pictures for comicbook versions of their most popular movie monster franchises.[11] The Code still explicitly forbade everything the Universal monsters were rooted in—as clearly stated in the Code's General Standards, Part B, "Scenes dealing with, or instruments associated with walking dead, torture, vampires and vampirism, ghouls, cannibalism, and werewolfism are prohibited". Thus, Dell alone could publish comics based on the Universal monsters. The monsters were about to become hot commercial properties, thanks to the forthcoming Aurora Model kits, which would enjoy record sales in 1962-63; the first, Frankenstein's Monster, hit shelves in the summer of 1962, joined by Dracula and the Wolfman by Christmas of that year. The monsters were already incredibly popular, thanks to the ongoing late-night TV broadcasts of the Screen Gems *Shock* and *Son of Shock* packages of Universal horror and monster movies in almost every American regional market, and the explosion of newsstand monster magazines led by *Famous Monsters of Filmland*. In terms of the comic book market, Dell was well ahead of the market wave, which had yet to crest. Dell's one-shot titles *Dracula, Frankenstein, The Wolf Man, The Mummy*, and *The Creature* hit the stands, and were instantaneous solid sellers (despite the fact that only *The Creature* offered an adaptation of the film property recognizable as such; the rest featured the monsters in stories that had precious little to do with the classic movies).

The mere concept of the walking dead embodied by characters like Frankenstein's monster and the Mummy was *verboten* by the Code, as was the vampirism central to *Dracula* and the lycanthropy (i.e., "werewolfism" in Code-speak) essential to *The Wolf Man*. Dell's *Dracula* comic flamboyantly flirted with breaking even more taboos. There was a page of imagery in *Dracula* explicitly forbidden by the Code: arms reaching out of open graves, a giant vampire bat carrying away a screaming victim, a mad scientist draining blood from a living victim into a skeleton (???), etc.

Arneson, Cole, and Stanley decided to push the envelope even further with *Ghost Stories* and *Tales from the Tomb*.

Which brings us, again, back to Dread End.

———

Another page turn brought seven-year-old me to page 4 of "The Monster of Dread End…," where we meet a boy dressed in red (including a snap-down red cap[12]) walking boldly onto the deserted streets of Dread End.

As if anything could possibly personalize the sense of suspense more, the caption to panel two reads, "Though only seven when his little sister became the first victim of the monster, Jimmy

---

9 William Jones notes, "Ruth A. Roche's adaptation of Mary Shelley's gothic parable remained one of Gilberton's most popular titles, going through 19 printings between 1945 and 1971" (Jones, *Classics Illustrated: A Cultural History, Second Edition*, pg. 51). The art for *Classics' Frankenstein* was by Robert Hayward Webb and Ann Brewster.

10 Precious few accurate records remain from the entire Western/Dell publishing empire, but for the purposes of this article, we'll go with the commonly acknowledged crediting to Arneson as editor of *Ghost Stories #1*, and Cole as editor of *Tales from the Tomb*. See http://comicbookdb.com/ issue.php?ID=128815 and http://comicbookdb.com/issue.php?ID=132034

11 Universal was also amid corporate changes at this time. Known as Universal-International throughout the 1950s, in 1962 Universal was taken over by the talent agency and TV production firm MCA (The Music Corporation of America) amid the MCA-Decca Records merger, and the studio was once again known as Universal Pictures; Universal City Studios, Inc. was formed in 1964. Note also that Dell contracted with Daystar Productions, the producers of *The Outer Limits*, to publish a comics series based on that soon-to-debut 1963 ABC-TV SF/horror TV series.

12 This coloring was smart storytelling, too: the red of Jimmy's cap and coat immediately visually linked Jimmy with the little girl who was jumping rope on page 1, panel 2 of the story. These kinds of color links are powerful tools, operating on a subconscious level for most readers.

White resolved that if the police didn't find her killer, some day he would…"

Damn. I was seven. I had a little sister (thankfully, I still do!).

This was really getting to me.

It's important that I leave something for you, dear reader, to enjoy when you read the story yourself.[13] Suffice to say that Jimmy spends two pages making his way to his and our first glimpse of the "Monster", and it's a doozy.

As a highly-skilled veteran writer/artist (Stanley had originally scripted and illustrated *Little Lulu* and Tubby, scripting *Little Lulu* and all *Lulu*-related titles from 1945-59, along with many other characters and titles), "Monster of Dread End…" author John Stanley was expert at story flow and how page turns work. It was a natural decision to provide our first teasing glimpse of the creature at the bottom of page 5, right at the page turn. Ed Robbins' artwork (likely working from page layouts provided by Stanley, who reportedly scripted in storyboard fashion, providing his creative partners with tight illustrative page designs) is ruthlessly efficient throughout. Robbins, too, was an industry veteran, having worked for many Golden Age comics publishers, beginning with *Marvel Mystery Comics*, working in all genres (including Pre-Code horror[14]) before eventually landing the Mickey Spillane *Mike Hammer* comic strip in the 1950s.

The collaborative chemistry between Stanley and Robbins is self-evident here, on page 5's final panel, though it's a deceptively simple image. At far left, we have Jimmy, turning away from us, deep in shadow (colored blue), looking out of the alley he's in towards something stirring in the street. Robbins renders Jimmy with slashes of black ink, the brick alley wall rendered with straight pen lines following the lay of the bricks and mortar toward the sidewalk and street, the perspective lines of the sidewalk further pulling our eye to the scuttling thing at the far right. At the end of the

Ed Robbins art, *Ghost Stories* #1, story page 6. Note Robbins' dynamic staging of the final panel, similar to that which ended page 5 (described in the article).

alley, on the street, there's an overturned garbage can, its shadows deep and pitch-black, its metal contours more emphatically directing us to—

—what appears to be a taloned hand, lifting a heavy metal manhole cover.

Just beyond this claw is the building across the street, a doorway framed by two darkened windows; the vertical forms and interior exclamation-mark-like splashes of ink pulling the eye down to the claw furtively scrabbling its way up from the sewers. It is neatly framed beneath the second window, the last object we will see on the page, at the point of turning the page.

Perfect.

And with the turn of the page, "The Monster of Dread End…" tips into real horror.

Jimmy watches as a seemingly boneless, bendable, possibly interminable serpentine "arm" slithers out of the manhole, over the street, and up the building's exterior wall, the spidery claw groping for another victim.

Now, even at the age of seven, I'd read and seen a lot of monster comics. I was a Monster Kid, all the

13 You can read it yourself online at *http://thehorrorsofitall. blogspot.com/2009/08/monster-of-dread-end.html*
14 Specifically, various stories for Stanley Morse/Key Publications' *Mister Mystery* (1952-1954) and *Weird Mysteries* (1953-1954), and for Martin Goodman's Atlas/ Timely line Robbins penciled and inked "The Man Who Cried Ghost" in *Adventures in Terror* #12 (October 1952), "The Bookworms" in *Journey into Unknown Worlds* #13 (October 1952), "A Thousand Years" in *Astonishing* #19 (November 1952), and, according to some sources, "By the Light of the Moon" for *Suspense* #29 (April 1953). Robbins later drew horror-mystery stories for DC's *The Unexpected* (1969) and for Western/Gold Key's *The Twilight Zone* (1970-1971), *Grimm's Ghost Stories* (#30, May 1976) and *Boris Karloff's Tales of Mystery* (#65, December 1975).

way, already assembling my first Universal Monster model and scouring newsstands for copies of *Famous Monsters of Filmland* and anything remotely like it. I'd cut my teeth on the mind-blowing Jack Kirby and Steve Ditko and Dick Ayers and Don Heck Atlas/Timely monster comics; I'd devoured every Dell Movie Comic with a dinosaur or monster, and spent hours in the Waterbury Public Library reading mythology books, with a refined taste already for the older hardcover myth text written by Padraic Colum and illustrated by Willy Pogany née Vilmos Andreas Pogány (*The Children of Odin, The Adventures of Odysseus and the Tale of Troy*, and my personal favorite, *The Golden Fleece*). I knew I hadn't seen or read it all—every issue of *Famous Monsters* let me know *how* little I'd seen or knew—but I'd seen and read a great many.

But I'd never seen or imagined anything like *this*.

Jack Kirby's monsters were almost always raging male expressions of vast size and power, while Steve Ditko's were all that (especially in the pages of *Gorgo* and *Konga*) and more. Ditko's comics creatures were usually associated with more devious parables about illusion vs. reality, insidious infiltration, misperception and the bizarre. Feeding habits weren't entirely invisible, either: the gaping jaws of Kirby's monsters were indicative of primal appetites and urges, just as Ditko's Gorgo and his mother were casually shown devouring fistfuls of sea life (fish, squids, etc.) and Konga's dietary needs were often detailed.

But the carnal appetite of the "claw" of Dread End struck a deeper nerve, evocative of a more obscene ravenous hunger. Fusing humanoid (the hand), serpentine, and arachnid (the spidery talons, the method of exsanguinating its prey) forms, the Dread End Monster placed the reader at the bottom of the food chain in ways the Code simply hadn't permitted since 1954. The connect-the-atrocities "dots" of John Stanley's script equated the night and open bedroom windows (which could be easily burst asunder even when attentive parents boarded them up) with an imaginary, stealthy, silent *thing* that slid into your room

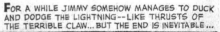

to seize and suck you dry in your sleep.

And in the morning, all that they'd find was something vaguely resembling a wad of tissue paper.

This—*this* was beyond weird.

This was *nasty*.

This was worse than anything I'd ever seen on a page.

This was something I just couldn't get my head around.

This was troubling in ways I'd never known monsters to be troubling.

What the hell *was* it? What was it *connected* to? How much more of it was down there, *under the streets?* How did it *feed* (oh, we find out!)? *How could you kill it? COULD you kill it??*

This was—

I won't give away any more of the story.

It's too short and simple and direct and sweet to spoil—

—save to acknowledge:

1. We never see what, if anything, the "arm" is attached to. Even after the final page of the story, we are left to wonder what the hell could have, might have, must have been below.

2. The terror grows, cumulatively, panel by panel, page by page, to the final page turn, never letting up until Stanley and Robbins have (pardon my French) "shot their load".

3. The finale necessarily involved one of the goriest images I'd ever seen in my young life up to that point in time.

Now, it's worth noting (and to my knowledge, nobody has in print before) that Dell Comics would be getting much more *direct* than any other 1960s mainstream four-color comicbook publisher in their occasional eruptions of mayhem. It was fleeting, the explicit imagery, but it was there. As a devotee of Sam Glanzman's comics for Dell, even as a kid, it was apparent in panels of *Kona Monarch of Monster Isle,* as the white-haired Cro-Magnon hero slashed into saurian and monster flesh with his bayonet. Sam's naturalistic approach to such violence was unusually frank: it wasn't gory, per se, though Kona did end up splashed with black (never red) blood in his most physical confrontations. This naturalism in depicting injury and death was even more apparent in Glanzman's harrowing *Combat* stories for Dell,

which were the first war comics of their generation to show us what war looked like. Having actively served in the U.S. Navy's Pacific theater during World War 2, Sam showed us what white-hot gunfire looked like when it was fired right *at* you; what it felt like when men were shot, and when planes erupted in flames with pilots trapped in the cockpits; and how sailors burned below molten decks as battleships were torpedoed and exploded. There was nothing sensationalistic or exploitative about Sam's depictions of violence: they just happened, they were *there*, clear on the page.

But that was after 1962: at the time "The Monster of Dread End..." was published, it was the most explicitly violent imagery I'd ever see in a four-color comic until the 1970s. For that matter, it was the most horrific imagery I'd lay eyes upon until the arrival a couple of years later of black-and-white horror comics like *Creepy* and *Eerie*, and, above all, Eerie Publications' Pre-Code reprint title *Weird*. The ending of "The Monster of Dread End..." was the most horrific thing I'd see in *any* comic for quite some time.

Terrible as that was, it didn't diminish the dread and horror of what Stanley and Robbins didn't show us: "a balled-up thing...like an empty wrapper..."

This was a lesson, too, in show and tell:

This was a lesson in what to show, and what to tell, in the telling of a horror story—the power of the unseen, the power of the seen, and the necessity of showing what could never be adequately described.

This wasn't just magic.

This was black magic, of the highest order: comics black magic, alchemy, genius.

I enjoyed and shivered over and read and reread the rest of *Ghost Stories* #1, time and time again. But the rest was pretty weak tea after that first story.

John Stanley and Ed Robbins collaborated on the next tale, "The Werewolf Wasp", another monster story of sorts. A geeky misfit with glasses (like me) has jarred an outsized wasp (just like I used to catch bees in a jar with my friends), and decides to take it over to "Professor Larvay". He'll know what it is!" He sure will, and he sure does, and thereby hangs the tale.

It's a silly trifle, really, but once again Stanley and Robbins pull the reader in and play the spider card to the max. I've already said too much; only later would I read stories like E.F. Benson's "Caterpillars" and John B.L. Goodwin's "The Cocoon" and recognize possible wellsprings for Stanley's story concept. Later still, in the 1980s, I would recognize a kindred spirit in Charles Burns and his first-published comics stories, which seemed to owe as much of a debt to Benson and Goodwin as "The Werewolf Wasp" did, in far more adult terms.

The last two stories in the comic, "The Door..." (artist unknown) and "The Black Stallion" (previously mentioned, with artwork by Gerald McCann) were effectively enigmatic. The former is a *Twilight Zone*-like fragment of a story, really, building to an open ending that's circular in design, bringing us back to the beginning in its way. This was the kind of story Stan Lee and Steve Ditko had been doing in the Atlas/Timely SF/fantasy comics I'd already been reading for a couple of years, and it neither puzzled nor scared me. "The Black Stallion" was more aggressive: a ghostly black horse with blazing red eyes, a fatal confrontation with the damned stallion during a violent lightening storm that finds its two boy protagonists fleeing into the upper loft of a barn the creature kicks to pieces, and another child death (Stanley knew what would shock younger readers: a glimpse of our own mortality!). In the end, "The Black Stallion" was the only real "ghost story" of the batch.

There were also the inside-cover black-and-white one-pagers by Stanley and McCann, slight confections that were "ghostly" enough (though the inside-back-covers had an overt science-fiction play with the form, set in outer space). I frankly can't recall if my copy sported advertising on the back cover, or instead featured the full-color one-pager by Stanley and McCann entitled "The Phantom Horse" (yep, another ghost horse story!). Some copies of *Ghost Stories* #1 had "The Phantom Horse", some didn't. I now have copies of *both* editions in my collection: one intended for subscribers, one for the newsstand. Given how central mail-order subscriptions were to Dell's marketing in the 1940s and 1950s, I'm fairly certain that explains why *Ghost Stories* #1 sports two different back covers, though only a few comics scholars like Robert Beerbohm have pondered the import of subscriptions to Dell's sales.

But those all faded from view, even as I read them.

I kept going back to Dread End—to shiver and marvel at that thing sliding up from the sewers.

It teased my waking days; it colored my darkest nights.

It was the scariest monster, ever.

And as surely as a hand crooking a finger to beckon me, it kept calling me back to the pages of *Ghost Stories...*

Ghosts? *Bah!*

This was worse than any ghost!

———

"The Monster of Dread End..." was reprinted twice by Dell: barely a year later, in Dell's 're-print-while-the-horror-is-hot' one-shot 'annual' *Universal Pictures Presents Dracula, The Mummy, and Other Stories* (1963), and five years later in a complete reprint, cover and all, of *Ghost Stories'* debut issue as *Ghost Stories* #21 (October 1968).

The latter remains the most affordable means of getting your hands on an original Dell printing of the story, for those hoping to hold the four-color original in their talons.

And then—it was forgotten, for the most part.

Dell's fortunes were waning by 1968, and horror in all media was exploding in more vivid, violent, and explicit directions. It was the year of **ROSEMARY'S BABY**, **NIGHT OF THE LIVING DEAD**, and **WITCHFINDER GENERAL / THE CONQUEROR WORM**, among a plethora of big-screen taboo-busters. Horror comics were thriving on the newsstands as the Warren and the Eerie Publications black-and-white horror comics 'zines flowed monthly and the Comics Code Authority continued to loosen its grip on the reins...

But for at least one lad growing up amid this horror boom, The Monster of Dread End never loosened its grip, and never left my daydreams, or my nightmares.

Especially when I was feeling *alone...*

———

It wasn't until I began appearing at comicbook conventions as a professional in the late-1970s and 1980s that I discovered I wasn't alone.

In short order, I discovered in almost every conversation with professionals in my age group that "The Monster of Dread End..." had scarred many an impressionable budding cartoonist. From fellow horror comics creators to *sui generis* innovators like Jaime and Gilbert Hernandez (famed creators of *Love and Rockets*, who also shared a love for the 1955 film **NIGHT OF THE HUNTER**), we'd all had an encounter with the enigmatic long arm of the (c)law in the pages of *Ghost Stories* #1. Like many an episode of *The Twilight Zone* and *The Outer Limits*, not everyone could recall *where* they'd seen or read that story. Many associated it with titles and publishers more commonly associated with horror—only a few remembered it was a Dell comic, fewer still which one, and almost none of us knew who had written or drawn the tale.

Comics creator Peter Von Sholly is a peer, a friend, a contemporary, and a creative confederate, too. He vividly remembers his first reading of "The Monster of Dread End…"—and he has done more than anyone to date to rekindle and resurrect those memories.

"I was twelve," Pete recalls. "The whole comic was weird and scary actually, the really juicy stuff happening 'offscreen' but 'Dread End' was the scariest comic story I'd ever read. The reveal of the monster was unforgettable! So weird."[15]

Decades later, while artists like myself were tinkering with swamp monsters and dinosaurs, Pete busied himself with storyboarding movies, creating novel trading card series, and creating comics. Among the second wave of comics creators to integrate digital technologies into his comics work, Pete launched a wild run of horror comics stories that plundered his love of the now-classic, old-fashioned "monster comics" of his youth. In the process, Pete remembered the frisson that first issue of Dell's *Ghost Stories* had delivered.

"When I started experimenting with my 'digi-metti' comics (*fumetti*[16] using Photoshop) it *then* occurred to me to try and re-do 'Dread End'." Once that was decided, Von Sholly got to work.

"I had a model of 'The Claw' custom-made and cast friends in the roles, plus shot plates on the backlot at one of the studios which I had access to at the time". This was the 20th Century-Fox studios *faux*-New York City backlot set, which we've all seen in literally hundreds of motion picture features and TV shows, including **HELLO, DOLLY**, **SPIDER-MAN**, **BATMAN**'s Gotham City, *Friends*, and *NYPD Blue*.[17]

The custom-made "Claw" was created by "a talented but strange sculptor (now deceased) named Mike Jones", and it was a rigid sculpture, not a flexible model. It remains an impressive creation when seen apart from the narrative context of Pete's adaptation of the John Stanley/Ed Robbins story.[18]

When I asked Pete if he worked up his initial draft of the story working strictly from memory, or based his layouts on a rereading and study of the original John Stanley/Ed Robbins story, Pete replied, "Both. I did try to replicate a couple of the most outstanding moments and compositions as close as I could. You know, like if 'Dread End' was a movie, what would it look like? I like the art in the comic for the most part, and in certain panels like when the claw crushes the trashcan you can almost *see* Stanley's layouts!"

"I didn't want to do a super-strict adaption, so I embellished a bit. I wanted to *show* more than

---

15 All quotes and inside information here is from the author's interview with Pete von Sholly, conducted on October 4-6, 2014, quoted here with permission.

16 Americans habitually refer to "photo comics" as *fumetti*, though that's technically incorrect. *Fumetti* or *fumetto* (singular form)—Italian for "little smoke", referencing word balloons—is the term Italy applies to *all* comics; in Italy, Europe, and most countries, what we call "photo comics" are referred to as *photo-romans* or *roman-photo* ("photo romances").

17 See *http://www.foxstudios.com/stages_exteriors/new_york_street.html*

18 Pete also noted, in an October 20th, 2014 email to me, "… my impression (when I first read 'Dread End') was that on the last page, we could see that the monster's body diminished in girth toward the "tail end" and that it did have an end. The monster didn't go on forever, which made it seem more plausible to me. Since they explained how it fed and so on—it was a physical creature, not something supernatural. It looks in the picture like it ends in a tapering tail as it goes down the manhole, to me."

Stanley [and Robbins] did in the comic, hence the nightmare scene and the added ending. … I added the things I wanted. Just about anything was viable in the digital world. I wanted to see the balled up corpse and so on".

Still, there were elements Pete wanted to keep in the shadows: "I didn't want to destroy the mystery which I think is part of the nightmarish charm of Stanley's horror and much good horror, that is to over-explain. All I wanted to do was go beneath the street to discover there was a whole lot more down where the Claw came from".

Pete's "remake" anticipated and arguably spurred a wave of similar creator "remakes" of beloved vintage comics stories—Paul Pope's reworking of Jack Kirby's debut issue of *Omac* in *Solo* #3 (DC Comics, 2005)[19], Kevin Huizenga's redrawing of the Charlton Comics 1956 *Mysteries of Unexplored Worlds* #6 story "The Half Men" in *Kramers Ergot* #8 (2012) and revamp of *Kona Monarch of Monster Isle* #1 as *Bona* in the self-published *The Half Men* (2013)[20], etc.[21] Now, thanks to Paul

and Kevin, it's a hip thing to do!

Though Pete and "Dread End" haven't received their due, Pete's inventive revamp of the Stanley/Robbins story remains a catalytic pioneer outing in this wave, and a potent read.

Ever humble, Pete says, "Looking at it now I think I could have done better, but so it goes!"

When asked if he had been similarly tempted to adapt any of the other John Stanley-scripted stories from *Ghost Stories* #1, Pete said, "I love 'The Werewolf Wasp', of course, and the one about the door ["The Door…", artist unknown], but I have not thought of adapting any others".

Pete's "remake" of "The Monster of Dread End…" has thus far appeared in three publications. "My version was published in the British mag *From the Tomb* [#12, February 2004] and in an anthology edited by Peter Normanton called *The Mammoth Book of Best Horror Comics* (which included the original version) [2008]… and also in my *Pete Von Sholly's Extremely Weird Stories* from Dark Horse (2006).[22] I had the enthusiastic support of John Stanley's son, James, and credited the rights to 'The John Stanley Estate'".

That's three printings to date, just like the Stanley/Robbins original story.

Thus, a new generation has been exposed to the thing that haunts Dread End: something sinister, something scaly, something *hungry*.

I wonder if they, too, will carry memories of the story—reprints of the John Stanley/Ed Robbins original, or now the Pete von Sholly adaptation—further into the 21st century.

The sun may never shine on Dread End, but in another way, the sun never sets on Dread End, either.

Not really.

Not ever.

And beneath Dread End, there lurks something more than mere darkness…

19 *See* http://paulpope.com/omac/

20 *See* http://fielder.tumblr.com/tagged/Bona1

21 Citing Kevin Huizenga and Tom Hart—not Pete von Sholly, silly folks—as their inspiration, there's more examples of comics pages redrawn by contemporary cartoonists up at the Tumblr "Redrawn" at *http://redrawncomics.tumblr.com/*

and of comicbook covers at "Covered" at *http://coveredblog. blogspot.com/* Of course, fans and fanzines have been doing the same thing since the 1960s, at least.

22 You can purchase *From the Tomb* #12 at *http:// fromthetombstore.synthasite.com/* and the two books reprinting the story are available from *amazon.com* and other online retailers.

Tales from the Tomb #1 (Dell Comics, 1962), cover art credited by many sources to L. B. Cole, who was art director at Dell at the time

MONSTER! #10 MOVIE CHECKLIST

MONSTER! Public Service posting: Title availability of films reviewed or mentioned in this issue of MONSTER!

Information dug up and presented by Steve Fenton and Tim Paxton.

The Fine Print: Unless otherwise noted, all Blu-rays and DVDs listed in this section are in the NTSC Region 1 format and widescreen, as well as coming complete with English dialogue (i.e., were either originally shot in that language, or else dubbed/subbed into it). If there are any deviations from the norm, such as full-frame format, discs from different regions or foreign-language dialogue (etc.), it shall be duly noted under the headings of the individual entries below.

Special Thanks to Dennis Capicik for giving us another invaluable assist with this ish's vid info. He always has lots of interesting details to add!

ABSURD (p.17) – Apparently, Shriek Show never actually released this domestically in a "Special Edition" (albeit presented full-frame) as **ANTRO-POPHAGUS II**, despite the rather convincing if phony-baloney-as-phuck DVD jacket bearing their brand name which I found via Google (at *www.dvd-covers.org*). Under that same title, however, X-Rated Kultvideo of Germany definitely did release it on VHS tape. It was also put out on NTSC Region 1 DVD by Mya Communication/Ryko in 2009 under the alternate title **HORRIBLE**, with Italian-or-English-dialogue audio options and no subs (at a 1.74:1 aspect ratio, but non-anamorphic). Under the present title, it was issued on British PAL Region 2 DVD in a "Collector's Edition" (I saw copies of said disc on offer at Seal Video [*www.sealvideo.co.uk*] for £9.99, but I can't say for sure whether it's a legit release or just a grey market DVD-R copy of Medusa's original 1981 VHS release [?]). In the same disc format in the same country, it has also been issued in a "Full Uncut Version" by the Visual-Pain co. (*www.visual-pain.co.uk*) as part of their irreverently/ironically-titled "Video Nasties Collectors Series" (ad: *"Brutal ...Shocking ...Violent ...Savage!"*). Once again, under the title **HORRIBLE** (its French title), it was released on DVD in France by Bach Films with Italian, French and English audio options and fullscreen only; Spain got it under the title **AB-SURD – TERROR SIN LIMITE** (*"Absurd – Unending Terror"*) from Trash Collectors, but it only had Italian and Spanish audio options, sans any English; in Germany it showed up as **ANTRO-POPHAGUS – DAS BIEST KEHRT ZURÜCK** (*"Antropophagus – The Beast Returns"*), and, although it was widescreen and enhanced for 16x9, it only had German audio. Entitled **MONSTER HUNTER**, way back in 1985 it was released on domestic North American VHS/Beta tape by Wizard Video (in a pan-and-scan fullscreen transfer print), packaged in a gaudy oversized box whose artwork—teeming with zombies!—had only the most tenuous connection to the actual movie itself,

but sure was eye-catching (as were many Wizard/Gorgon vid-boxes of the period). This very same version was later re-packaged on VHS by sell-thru specialists/rip-off artists T-Z Video under the title **ZOMBIE 6: MONSTER HUNTER**, which came in a cheapo slipcase cover.

ANTHROPOPHAGUS (p.15) – Ad-line: *"It's Not The Fear That Will Tear You Apart. It's Him"*. As **ANTHROPOPHAGUS: THE GRIM REAPER**, this was put out in a 2-disc special edition (at 1.66:1 aspect ratio [widescreen]) by Shriek Show/Media Blasters in 2006. Disc 2 of their loaded 2-disc special edition included the special documentary feature *Joe D'Amato – Totally Uncut Part Two* (in Italian with English subs); Part One of which was included with SS/MB's DVD release of Joe's notorious nudie nunsploitationer **IMAGES IN A CONVENT** (*Immagini di un convento*, 1979). The film was also put out on Italian DVD (1.66:1, with English option) by Beat Records in an edition likewise loaded to the 'nads with extra features. As **THE GRIM REAPER**, it was released (at 1.33:1 aspect ratio [fullscreen])

CASTLE OF BLOOD Spanish DVD

on NTSC All-Region DVD in 1998 by DVD Ltd. In 1984, Monterey Home Video (MHV) issued it on VHS videocassette (fullscreen) as **THE GRIM REAPER**, its bowdlerized and re-scored US version. As **ANTHROPOPHAGOUS: THE BEAST**, it was issued on VHS tape in the UK *circa* the '80s by Video Film Promotions (VFP), and it subsequently became added to the so-called "Video Nasty" witch hunters' short list in Britain. Bearing the Spanish title **ANTROPOFAGO** on the box—the transfer print of the film itself is in English, with Spanish subs and widescreen—it was issued on Venezuelan VHS cassette by VideoShow back in the '80s (in the same format and with the same specifications, it was also released in Venezuela under its original and bland English-language export title, **THE SAVAGE ISLAND**). As of this writing, there was one copy of said ultra-rare **ANTROPOFAGO** tape, complete with reconstructed box, up for auction on eBay...with a starting bid of a mere $399.00, for any millionaire *Monster!* readers who might be interested in owning/seeing it in a "dead" format of far lesser quality than certain digital versions that are readily available nowadays. Desert Island Discs of Italy has also issued it on DVD (in 2012); their cover art is evidently a reproduction of the box to the aforementioned MHV VHS version. A "Collector's Edition" DVD was released in Germany by XT Video Entertainment under the title **MAN-EATER** (also bearing the German box title **DER MENSCHEN-FRESSER**, given in parenthesis below the English

one). As of this writing it was up for sale at eBay (for $69.99, in a package deal with XT's deluxe edition of Jess Franco's **DEVIL HUNTER** [box title: **JUNGFRAU UNTER KANNIBALEN**]). Both discs are separately packaged in "Steelbooks with 3D Lenticular covers", and both come with English- as well as German-language audio options. In France, Bach Films released it on DVD as **ANTHROPOPHAGOUS** in widescreen (1.77:1 & 16x9) with Italian, French & English audio options; in Italy it was also released as a 2-disc set from Big Fish as **ANTROPOPHAGUS**, again in widescreen (1.85:1 & 16x9) with Italian, Spanish and English audio options. It also had numerous extras not found on Shriek Show's domestic disc, including soundtrack selections from many of Joe D'Amato's films and an on-set documentary/interview (shot by veteran Italian actress Malisa Longo!) from one of his late-'90s adult films. Lastly, back in the day MPA Video also released this on French-Canadian VHS in an eye-catching "Eastman-eating-his-own-guts" big box clamshell. It was in French only though.

CASTLE OF BLOOD (p.19) – Ad-line: *"The living and the dead change places in this orgy of terror!"* Released on domestic DVD in 2002 by Synapse Films in an "Uncensored International Version" (at 1.78:1), with a French-language audio track and English subs. In 2010, Sinister Cinema also put it out on DVD (fullscreen); their version is alternately available as an Amazon Instant Video (a mere $1.99 to rent in SD, and $7.99 to buy in the same picture quality format ["standard definition"]). In a presumably much grottier/gnarlier version—and fullscreen, yet—the film was put out on NTSC Region 1 DVD by the unlikely-sounding Family Value Collection, seemingly randomly double-billed with a copy of the Filipino schlocker **BLOOD THIRST** which I'm sure can't hold a candle to Vinegar Syndrome's gorgeous version (released in 2013) . As for **CASTLE OF BLOOD**, Synapse's version is about the best way to go, from the looks of it. It seems easy enough to get ahold of, as I saw a number of copies for sale at both Amazon and eBay. Something Weird Video (SWV) formerly sold it in the VHS format. There are several different uploads of the film on YouTube, as well as some trailers, including one for Woolner Brothers' US theatrical release (narrator: *"No one has ever witnessed and survived the awesome secrets; the ghostly events of this castle of the damned! ...Here, the dead rise from their tombs once a year, to repeat their hideous crimes of murder and passion! ...Edgar Allan Poe's most gripping, chilling drama of horror and suspense!"*).

CREATURE 3D (p.11) – Ad: *"Fear Has A New Face"*. Released on All-Region DVD (in Hindi, with English subs and 5.1 digital Dolby audio) by T-Series. I saw several listings for said disc on eBay, but the prices varied wildly, so shop wisely! I could find no listing for it on Amazon, but you can always check Induna's site (*www.induna. com*). T-Series also released an audio CD of this film's soundtrack, composed by Mithoon.

EVIL CAT (p.52) – Originally released on VHS/ Beta, back in the late '80s and '90s, it was available on tape in the US from the San Francisco-based Rainbow Audio & Video Corporation, in the original Chinese (w/ English subs?). It later became available on DVD from Fortune Star. A very watchable widescreen, English-subbed version is viewable on YouTube. Beware of the high-speed subs on the FS disc though, because they streak by quicker than a cat on speed; so be prepared to periodically hit pause or rewind in order to properly read the longer ones! **EC** has also been released on HK DVD by Media Asia Distribution / Mega Star Video Distribution, possibly with the same contents/format as Fortune Star's version (?).

GHOST OF SAGA MANSION (p.43, within the **KURONEKO** review) – Although it was released on DVD some years back by Japan's Kadokawa Video, their disc has since gone OOP. While I cannot locate the whole film there, there is an amazing 8½-minute excerpt— in Japanese, non-subtitled—from it on YouTube, for those interested in a tempting taster of this vintage (1953) "ghost-cat" *kaidan*. Unfortunately, about the only way you'll be able to access it is via the Japanese *kanji/hiragana/katakana* characters (i.e., 怪談佐賀屋敷), which is what the link is titled). The best way to go about it is to type either the English title or/and its Latin/Roman alphabet transliteration (*Kaidan Saga yashiki*) into search at Wikipedia; there's an entry for it there which includes the above Japanese characters. Simply copy-and-paste the *kanji* title over into search at YT and—*voila!*—you'll be in instant crazy kitty-critter heaven! If that sample doesn't make you wanna see more *kaibyō* ("ghost-cat") flicks, nothing will.

HALLOWEEN III: SEASON OF THE WITCH (p.21) – This title was originally released way back in 1998 at the start of the DVD revolution by the budget label Good Times in a decent (for its time) 2.35:1, non-anamorphic snap-case DVD. In 2007, Universal Video double-billed this in a 2-disc DVD set with **HALLOWEEN II** (as of this writing, there was a copy on eBay which had a starting bid of only $1.99!). Universal also put it out on DVD by its lonesome back in 2003. It has also been released on PAL Region B Blu in Germany (presumably with an English-language

audio option?) by NSM Records. Their limited edition comes packaged in a "Blu-ray Metalpak (similar to steelbook)", complete with a "Lenticular 3D Hologram Cover" (featuring all-new artwork). As of this writing, a copy of said version was on offer at eBay for $104.99, so if you really need all the bells and whistles, why not snap it up (although I'm not sure what special features— if any—NSM's edition comes with). The same company also put it out in a Mediabook edition containing not just Blu and DVD copies of the film, but a CD of its John Carpenter/Alan Howarth-composed soundtrack too. Unless you wanna pay through the nose, I'd say about the best way to go would be to pick up the 2012 Collector's Edition Blu-ray released by Shout! Factory (through their Scream Factory line): namely their "30th Anniversary 'Silver Shamrock' Edition", which includes numerous special features as well as snazzy all-new cover art. This title is readily available in a number of different formats (VHS and Amazon insta-vid included, natch!), so those who want it will have no trouble finding themselves a copy that best fits their requirements. For the more dedicated collector of **H3: SOTW** memorabilia, I saw a ton of paper promo materials for sale online, as well as contemporary T-shirts and original Don Post "Silver Shamrock Novelties" masks (i.e., there was a Skull one on eBay for "only" $137.99).

HARIMAU JADIAN (p.49) – I found two different uploads of this ultra-obscure B&W Malaysian kitty-critter movie at YouTube: a full-length upload (bearing the constant yellow watermark "*Filem Klasik*"—guess what that means!—in its top right-hand corner) at the link entitled "*Harimau Jadian (1972) 578x360*", plus another in two parts, with slightly inferior picture quality if sans any watermark (@ "*harimau jadian 1*" and "*harimau jadian 2*"); both versions total around 85m. each and appear to have been ripped from the same original source (a VCD or TV airing, perhaps?). I've read at two different vaguely-worded online sources how P. Ramlee's "lost" 1964 weretiger movie **SITORA HARIMAU JADIAN** (p.57) has been released on Malaysian VCD by the native Music Valley company (who release a lot of Malay/Singaporean movies in said disc format), but this seems highly unlikely. What I've been thinking maybe is that the mentions I saw were simply erroneous (or just plain bogus), and that possibly the MV co. may actually have released this present 1972 title instead, either accidentally misrepresenting its title or possibly even intentionally doing so in hopes of generating better sales? (Assuming maybe that customers might order it, expecting it to be the Ramlee flick, then not bothering sending it back for a refund when

they found out they'd been gypped? A long-shot I know, but stranger things have happened in the sometimes shady, sleazy world of video exploitation.) Your guess is as good as mine, but if I find out that **SITORA** really *is* available on VCD from them, will I ever be eating crow, and a full retraction will be in order! ☺

KHOONI PANJA (p.5) – Released on Indian VCD by TNT (Time N Tune), who apparently also released it on DVD (if the listing at *www.webmallindia.com* is to be believed); TNT's disc comes in Hindi, without English subs. It was formerly available on Indian VHS tape from Excel Video. There is a 2-part, Hindi-language, non-subbed rip of the film—imprinted with a large watermark for "Bombino" in the top left-hand corner throughout—uploaded to YouTube. As of this writing, oddly enough, for some reason the second part of the film at YT had totaled roughly three times as many views as the first part (presumably because the viewers preferred to skip over all the boring stuff and cut straight to the chase?).

KURONEKO (p.42) – Released on DVD as part of the Criterion Collection (2011), it was also put out in the same format by Eureka! in 2005 as part

of their "The Masters of Cinema Series". In 2010, it was given a theatrical rerelease by Janus Films. There are multiple options available to view this well-known and highly-regarded film, so it's easy enough to do for those who want to see it badly enough (and if you *don't*, you *should*). Something Weird Video (SWV) issued it on NTSC VHS in the USA, and back in 1983 Palace Video did likewise on PAL VHS in the UK. In 1995, it was also released in that same format by the UK's Tartan Video too, but they evidently never put it out in digital disc format.

THE NIGHT STALKER (p.36) & **THE NIGHT STRANGLER** (p.38) – Although that former title had been put out on VHS tape by Magnum Entertainment circa the late-'80s ('90s?), it was first issued on domestic DVD by Anchor Bay Entertainment in 1998. In 2004, both **STALKER** and **STRANGLER** were released in much better-quality DVD form by Metro Goldwyn Mayer Home Entertainment (*www.mgm.com*) as a double-sided Double Feature disc. Special features consist of two documentary featurettes: one contains a close to 15-minute on-camera interview with Dan Curtis, specially-shot for this DVD edition; in the other (clocking-in at around 7½ minutes, including credits), Curtis discusses directing the latter title. Because both films were originally produced for the small screen, MGM's master transfer prints are naturally enough presented in their original full-frame aspect ratio, and the image quality is generally mighty fine indeed. Also, on a related note (even though original creator Curtis had no input into the show other than providing its inspiration source and creating its principal characters), back in 2005—I snagged myself one for Christmas that year for a mere $45 (Canadian)—Universal home vid released a 3-disc box DVD set of the *Kolchak: The Night Stalker* teleseries (1974-75), containing all 20 episodes of the short-lived show. While it still makes for a fun watch largely for fans of the timeless McGavin/Oakland love/hate interaction (those actors play off each other so wonderfully and with such impeccable timing, they're always a joy to behold, even when verbally tearing each other to shreds!), the show really started going downhill fast, but some of the individual episodes are still great, even if the series as a whole was better off ending at an even score of episodes rather than getting to the point where they were flogging a dead horse. Uni's *Kolchak* DVD set includes no extras, but the presentation and packaging are quite nice. It's also great fun spotting all the guest stars and supporting actors who pop up throughout the run of the series. Even if some of the monsters are rather on the cheesy side, there are some great ones mixed in too, as well as some pretty decent storylines, so if you do ever get a chance to grab the set for a good price, by all means snap it up! On a related note of Curtisiana, in 2012 MPI Home Video released a "Deluxe Edition"—*and then some!*—DVD mega-set entitled *Dark Shadows: The Complete Original Series*, packaged in a coffin-shaped box. A mind-boggling *470* hours (!!!) in total running time, numbering *1,225* (!!!) episodes on *131* discs (!!!), as well as more than 120 bonus cast and crew video interviews, plus about ten-gazillion other extras besides (give or take a few million). As of this writing at Amazon, this monster of a set—whose list price is a suitably monstrous $599.98—was on offer for $349.96… that's a saving of $250.02 (needless to say, only ultra-fucking-hardcore *DS* maniacs need apply!). I would gladly watch a number of select episodes, but I don't have enough damn life left to me to "waste" sitting through the whole lot—that's a grand total of 19 days and 14 hours, if watched continuously; and that's not even including all the supplemental material! But kudos to MPI for even attempting such a vast undertaking, let alone actually achieving it. I'm sure it has to have broken some sort of record for a home video release.

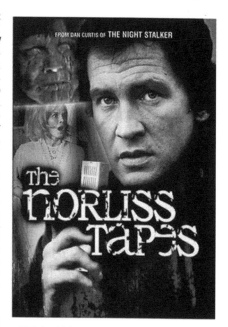

THE NORLISS TAPES (p.32) – Put out in 2006 on homegrown DVD by Starz/Anchor Bay Entertainment in a spartan "no-frills" edition (i.e., without any special features whatsoever), albeit with very decent picture quality. Due to being made for television, the print is presented at its proper original screen dimensions (full-frame). On an indirectly related note, interestingly enough, while Googling for this title I ran across a link to a site offering audio downloads of music for a current Swedish band (solo artist?) calling themselves… *The Norliss Tapes!* I forgot to copy and paste the URL addy, but I'm sure their stuff's easy enough to find online for those interested in finding out what it's like. I saw a number of "records" on offer at said site (I think it might have been at *bandcamp.com*), including one, complete with bright orange "pumpkinhead" cover art, entitled (topically enough for this time of year!) *It's Halloween*, and another—a 5-song e.p.—was entitled *Bad Robot*. A description at their site calls their stuff "space-age garage lounge music". I haven't heard any of their material, but that description sounds interesting enough to make me curious.

THE PLAGUE OF THE ZOMBIES & THE REPTILE (p.25) – At the end of his joint review of the films on p.29, Troy Howarth goes into some detail about the recent PAL Region B Blu-ray releases of these two mandatory Hammer classics. Both films were first released on US DVD and VHS by Anchor Bay Entertainment in 1999. They were subsequently rereleased by Anchor Bay in 2003 as 2-disc sets, respectively paired-up

with John Gilling's **THE MUMMY'S SHROUD** (1967) and Michael Carreras' loopy monster fantasy **THE LOST CONTINENT** (1968). In the UK, Optimum Releasing also released both titles on PAL Region B disc as part of their "Hammer Collection". All of the above releases were widescreen (1.66:1) and 16x9 enhanced. In 2013, the Shock label out of Australia also released both **PLAGUE** and **REPTILE** as "Double Play" Region B Blu ("Fully restored on Blu-ray for the first time") / DVD combos.

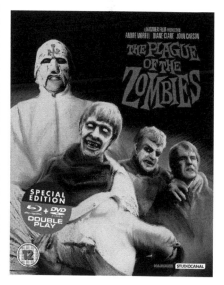

8231658R00061

Printed in Great Britain
by Amazon.co.uk, Ltd.,
Marston Gate.